ENGLISH GRAMMAR
FOR
STUDENTS OF FRENCH

JACQUELINE MORTON

WAYNE STATE UNIVERSITY

The Olivia and Hill Press, Inc.
P.O. Box 7396
Ann Arbor, Michigan 48107

English Grammar series
edited by Jacqueline Morton

English Grammar for Students of French
English Grammar for Students of Spanish
English Grammar for Students of German
English Grammar for Students of Latin (forthcoming)

<< In Preparation >>

English Grammar for Students of Italian
English Grammar for Students of Russian

© 1979 by Brian N. and Jacqueline Morton

Printed in the U.S.A.

Library of Congress Catalog Card Number: 79-87578
ISBN   0-934034-00-1

< < Contents > >

< < To the Student > >

As you have probably discovered, your French grammar book refers to a number of grammatical terms, such as conjugation, pronouns, direct and indirect objects and many others. Although you may have heard of these terms before, you may not be sure of what they mean. You do not have to know how to identify parts of speech and the function of words in order to write English correctly, but you will have to know this in order to learn French.

This handbook explains grammatical concepts in simple English, gives many examples in English, and then shows you step by step how to apply them to French. *English Grammar for Students of French* is not meant to replace your French book but rather to help you get the most out of it. Since this is one book in which you are encouraged to write, spaces have been provided for notes.

< < To the Teacher > >

This self-study manual is intended for high school and college students beginning the study of French. As you are well aware, many of them have never been taught to identify parts of speech or to analyze the function of words in an English sentence. Without this basic knowedge, the students are severely handicapped in learning a foreign language. *English Grammar for Students of French* defines common grammatical concepts in a way particularly suited for students learning French. It assumes no knowledge of English grammar and is designed to supplement any beginning French textbook. Certain key French and English structures have been singled out for a point-by-point comparison. Exceptions to French grammatical rules, as well as those points which have no English equivalents, have purposely been omitted. For easy reference, there is a detailed word index.

While this book is directed to students, you, the teacher, may find that the examples presented and the contrastive analyses given will save you time in preparing lessons.

This text has already been used most effectively by students, teaching assistants and language teachers at Wayne State University.

Jacqueline Morton

Ann Arbor, Michigan
May, 1979

< < About the Author > >

Jacqueline Morton was born in France and received her M.A. and Ph.D. from Columbia University in New York. She has taught French at Columbia University and at Smith College (Mass.), and English at the Ecole supérieure de Commerce et d'Administration in Paris and in Marseilles. She is currently Coordinator of French Basic Courses at Wayne State University.

She has published three French readers: *La Presse* and *La Presse II* (D.C. Heath) which she co-authored with Brian N. Morton of the University of Michigan, and *Mosaïque* (Van Nostrand) in collaboration with Michio P. Hagiwara also of the University of Michigan.

Her scholarly publications include *La Correspondance d'André Gide et de François Mauriac* (Gallimard) and *La Correspondance d'André Gide et de Justin O'Brien* (Société des études gidiennes). She is currently working on a major study of André Gide as a translator.

<< Introduction >>

When you learn a foreign language, in this case French, you must look at each word in three ways:

1. The **meaning** of the word—an English word must be connected with a French word which has an equivalent meaning.

> *Boy,* a young male child, has the same
> meaning as the French word **garçon.**

Words with equivalent meanings are learned by memorizing **vocabulary** items. Each word of the vocabulary must be learned separately; rarely will knowing one French word help you to learn another one.

> Knowing that *boy* is **garçon** will not
> help you to learn that **fille** is *girl.*

2. The **form** of the word—English and French words are classified according to **part of speech.** There are eight different parts of speech:

noun	article
verb	adverb
pronoun	preposition
adjective	conjunction

Each part of speech has its own rules for spelling, pronunciation, and use. You must learn to recognize what part of speech a word belongs to in order to choose the correct French equivalent and know what rules for spelling and pronunciation apply.

1

2

Look at the word *what* in the following sentences:

    a. *What* do you want?
    b. *What* movie do you want to see?
    c. I'll do *what* you want.[1]

The English word is the same; but in French three different words will be used and three different rules will apply, because each *what* belongs to a different part of speech.

3. The **use** of the word—a word must be identified according to the role it plays in the sentence. Each word, whether English or French, plays a specific role. Determining this role or **function** will also help you to choose the correct French equivalent and to know what rules apply.

Let us go back again to the word *what*. You need to identify the role it plays in the following sentences:

    a. *What* is on the table?
    b. *What* is she doing?
    c. *What* are you talking about?[2]

Because *what* plays a different role in each sentence above, its French equivalent will be different in each sentence.

NOTE: As a student of French you must learn to recognize parts of speech and determine function of words in a given sentence. This is essential because in French words in a sentence have a great deal of influence one over the other.

Compare this sentence in English and in French:

*The small black **shoes** are on the big round table.*

Les petites **chaussures** noires sont sur la grande **table** ronde.

---

[1] a. Interrogative pronoun – see p. 103.
  b. Interrogative adjective – see p. 75.
  c. Relative pronoun without antecedent – see p. 136.
[2] a. Subject – see p. 20.
  b. Direct object – see p. 86.
  c. Object of a preposition – see p. 89.

In English: The only word that affects another word in the sentence is *shoes*, which affects *are*. If the word were *shoe*, *are* would be *is*.

In French: The word for *shoes* (**chaussures**) not only affects *are* but also the spelling and pronunciation of the equivalent word for *the, small,* and *black*.

The word for *table* (**table**) affects the spelling and pronunciation of the equivalent words for *the, big,* and *round*.

The only word which is not affected by the words surrounding it is **sur**, which means *on*.

Since parts of speech and function are usually determined in the same way in English and in French, this handbook will show you how to identify them in English. You will then learn to compare English and French constructions. This will give you a better understanding of the explanations in your French grammar book.

<< **What is a Noun?** >>

A **noun** is a word that can be the name of:

- a person   Mary, Smith, Bozo, professor, clown
- a place   Detroit, Michigan, United States, city, state, country, continent
- a thing or animal lamp, airplane, sky, dog, cat, bird
- an idea   peace, war, democracy, love, grief

Nouns that always begin with a capital letter, such as the names of people and places (Mary, Mr. Smith, Michigan), are called **proper nouns**. Nouns that do not begin with a capital letter (peace, professor, dog) are called **common nouns**.

4

To help you learn to recognize nouns, here is a paragraph where the nouns are in italics:

> The best *purchases* from *France* include *wines, perfumes, scarves, gloves* and other luxury *items*. Today, French *workmen* make excellent *skis* and tennis[1] *rackets* which are sold the *world* over. Thanks to the *Common Market*, you can find *goods* from *Germany, Italy, England* and their *partners* in all large French *stores*. Thus, Italian *sportscars*, English leather[1] *goods*, German *glassware* and Belgian *lace* can be bought at *prices* comparable to those in the *country* of *origin*.

<<   What is Meant by Gender?   >>

When a word can be classified as to whether it is **masculine, feminine,** or **neuter**, it is said to have a **gender**.

Gender plays a very small role in English; however, since it is at the very heart of the French language, let us see what evidence of gender we have in English.

In English: When we use a noun we often do not realize that it has a gender. But when we replace the noun with *he, she,* or *it,* we choose only one of the three without hesitation because we automatically give a gender to the noun we are replacing. The gender corresponds to the sex of the person we are replacing.

> The *boy* came home; *he* was tired and I was glad to see *him.*

> A noun (*boy*) is of the **masculine gender** if *he* or *him* is used to substitute for it.

---

[1] This is an example of a noun used as an adjective; that is, to describe another noun. See p. 69.

My *aunt* came for a visit; *she* is nice and I like *her*.

A noun (*aunt*) is of the **feminine gender** if *she* or *her* is used to substitute for it.

There is a *tree* in front of the house. *It* is a Maple.

A noun (*tree*) is of the **neuter gender** if *it* is substituted for it.[1]

In French: All nouns, common nouns and proper nouns, are either masculine or feminine. There is no such thing as a neuter noun. This means that all objects, animals, and abstract ideas have a gender, as have the names of countries. Unlike English, where the few examples of gender are based on the sex of the noun, gender in French cannot be explained or figured out. It is a question of the French language itself.

Examples of English nouns whose equivalents are *masculine* in French:	Examples of English nouns whose equivalents are *feminine* in French:
boat	car
book	library
vice	virtue
suicide	death
Japan	France
professor (whether it refers to a man or woman)	childhood
	democracy
	strength
paradise	power

You will have to memorize each noun with its gender. This gender is important not only for the noun itself, but for the spelling and pronunciation of the words it influences.

Gender can sometimes be determined by looking at the ending of a noun. Below are some noun endings which often correspond to the masculine gender and others

---

[1] There are a few well-known exceptions, such as *ship*, which is referred to as *she*. It is custom, not logic, which decides.

The S/S United States sailed for Europe. She is a beautiful ship.

6

which correspond to the feminine gender.[1] Since you will encounter many nouns with these endings in basic French, it is certainly worth your familiarizing yourself with them.

Masculine Endings

-age	village, potage, collage
-al	journal, animal, hôpital
-at	chocolat, consulat, baccalauréat
-eau	tableau, chapeau, bateau
-ent	président, client, patient
-er	déjeuner, dîner, souper
	menuisier, boulanger, boucher *(trades)*
	poirier, oranger, pommier *(trees)*
-et	objet, sujet, projet
-eur	vendeur, porteur, chanteur *(trades)*
	moteur, radiateur, calculateur *(devices)*
-ien	mécanicien, pharmacien, politicien
-in	cousin, voisin, médecin
-isme	communisme, nationalisme, optimisme
-oir	devoir, couloir, soir
-ment	gouvernement, appartement, monument

Feminine Endings

-ade	salade, marmelade, façade
-aine	fontaine, chaîne, laine
-aison	conjugaison, terminaison, maison
-ance	correspondance, dance, France
-ande	commande, demande, viande
-ée	soirée, journée, entrée
-eille	oreille, bouteille, corbeille
-ence	agence, présence, absence
-ère	boulangère, bouchère, menagère *(trades)*
-esse	maîtresse, hôtesse, politesse
-ette	fourchette, assiette, serviette
-eur	chaleur, horreur, couleur *(abstract)*
-euse	vendeuse, chanteuse, danseuse
-ie	économie, géographie, compagnie

---

[1]We thank Professor Michio Hagiwara and his publisher for authorization to reproduce this list from *Thème et Variations* (New York: John Wiley & Sons), 1977.

-ienne	comédienne, musicienne, canadienne
-ine	cousine, voisine, médecine
-ique	technique, musique, panique
-ise	valise, surprise, église
-oire	poire, victoire, histoire
-onne	personne, Sorbonne, bonne
-sion	télévision, mission, profession
-té	liberté, nationalité, bonté
-tion	question, nation, addition
-trice	actrice, directrice, monitrice
-tude	étude, solitude, attitude
-ure	voiture, culture, architecture

<<   What is Meant by Number?   >>

When a word refers to one person or thing, it is said to be **singular**; when it refers to more than one, it is called **plural**.

Some nouns, called **collective nouns,** refer to a group of persons or things, but they are considered singular.

> A football *team* has eleven players.
> The *family* is well.
> The *crowd* was under control.

In English: We indicate the plural in a few ways:

- by adding an *-s* or *-es* to a singular noun

    book → book*s*
    kiss → kiss*es*

- sometimes by making a spelling change

    m*an* → m*en*
    lea*f* → lea*ves*

A plural noun is usually spelled differently and sounds different from the singular.

In French: A word in the plural is usually spelled differently from the singular. The most common change is the same one made as in English; that is, an -s is added to the singular noun.

> livre → livres
> table → tables

The main difference between English and French is that even though you can <u>see</u> the plural if you are reading the word, you can rarely <u>hear</u> that the word is plural because the final "s" is not pronounced.[1]

---

livre (sing.)		table (sing.)
	same pronunciation	
livre**s** (pl.)		table**s** (pl.)

You have to listen to the word that comes <u>before</u> the noun to know whether the noun is singular or plural.

NOTE: Nouns do not change gender when they become plural.

Compare where you <u>hear</u> the plural in

English	*French*
the book (sing.)	le livre (sing.)
the books (pl.)	**les** livres (pl.)

In English: You hear the plural in the noun itself.

In French: You often hear it only in the definite or indefinite article which comes before the noun.

---

[1]The most common exception to this rule are nouns ending in -al in the singular and which change to -aux in the plural. Ex.: **journal** (sing.), **journaux** (pl.); **animal** (sing.), **animaux** (pl.).

<< What are Indefinite and Definite Articles? >>

The **article** is a word which is placed before a noun to show if the noun refers to a particular person, thing, animal or object or if the noun refers to an unspecified person, thing, animal or object.

In English: A. **Indefinite Articles**

A or *an* is used before a noun when we do not speak of a particular person, thing, animal or object. They are called indefinite articles.

I saw *a* boy in the street.
(not a particular boy)

I ate *an* apple.
(not a particular apple)

The indefinite article is used only with a singular noun; it is dropped when the noun becomes plural. Sometimes the word *some* is used to replace it.

I saw boys in the street.
I saw *some* boys in the street.

I ate apples.
I ate *some* apples.

B. **Definite Articles**

The is used before a noun when we are speaking of a particular person, thing, animal or object. It is called the definite article.

I saw *the* boy you spoke to me about.
(a particular boy)

I ate *the* apple you gave me.
(a particular apple)

The definite article remains "the" when the noun becomes plural.

I saw *the boys* you spoke to me about.

I ate *the apples* you gave me.

In French: The article, definite or indefinite, has a much greater role than its English equivalent. It works hand in hand with the noun it belongs to in that it matches the noun's gender and number. This "matching" is called **agreement.** (One says that "the article agrees with the noun.") You use a different article depending on whether the noun is masculine or feminine, and depending on whether the noun is singular or plural. Because these articles are pronounced differently, they will indicate the gender and number of the noun to the ear.

A. Indefinite Articles

- **Un** indicates that the noun is masculine singular.

un livre	*a book*
un garçon	*a boy*

- **Une** indicates that the noun is feminine singular.

une table	*a table*
une pomme	*an apple*

Memorize French nouns with their *singular indefinite articles*. These articles do not change and will always tell you if the noun is masculine or feminine.

- **Des** indicates that the noun is plural; it does not tell you the gender since **des** is the plural for both masculine and feminine nouns.

des livres	(masc. pl.)	*books*
des garçons		*boys*
des tables	(fém. pl.)	*tables*
des pommes		*apples*

In written French you can see the plural in both the indefinite article des and in the noun *livres, garçons, tables*, and
pommes. In spoken French you will only be able to hear
the plural in the indefinite article des which comes before
the noun since the "s" of the plural is not pronounced.

NOTE: Although the plural indefinite article may be
dropped in English, it cannot be left out in French.

> *I saw boys in the street.*
>
> J'ai vu **des garçons** dans la rue.

> *I ate apples.*
>
> J'ai mangé **des pommes**.

B. Definite Articles

- **Le** indicates that the noun is masculine singular.

le livre	*the book*
le garçon	*the boy*

- **La** indicates that the noun is feminine singular.

la table	*the table*
la pomme	*the apple*

Although it's easy to see the difference between **le** and
la, its harder to hear the difference because the masculine **le** usually sounds like an "l" attached to the previous word.

Voilà le livre	sounds like	**Voilal livre*

---

*An asterisk means what follows is incorrect. It is merely an illustration.

It's easier, therefore, to listen for the feminine article **la** because the "a" is not dropped in pronunciation. If you hear the "a", you know that the noun that follows is feminine; if you don't hear the "a", assume that the article is **le** and that the noun following is masculine.

- **Les** indicates that the noun is plural; it does not tell you the gender since **les** is the plural for both masculine and feminine nouns.

les livres	(masc. pl.)	*the books*
les garçons		*the boys*
les tables	(fém. pl.)	*the tables*
les pommes		*the apples*

Here again, there is no problem in seeing the plural when you read these words; however, you will only be able to <u>hear</u> the plural in the plural definite article **les** that comes before the noun.

<< What is a Mute "H"? >>

In English: A **mute** (silent) **"h"** is an "h" that is not pronounced. Compare your pronunciation of:

Column 1	and	*Column 2*
hotel		hour
horse		honor
hat		heir

The "h" is pronounced in the words in Column 1; the "h" is silent in the words in Column 2. When the "h" is not pronounced, it is called a mute "h".

The indefinite article *an* (instead of *a*) is used before a mute "h": *an* hour, *an* honor, *an* heir.

13

In French: The letter "h" exists only in writing; it is never pronounced. In most cases, just ignore the "h" and consider the word as starting with a vowel.

> **Hôtel** and **herbe** are considered as starting with a vowel.

There are two important consequences:

1. In the singular, **le** and **la** change to **l'**. The dropping of a final vowel before a word starting with a vowel is called an **elision**.

> *le hôtel → l'hôtel (*the hotel*)
> *la herbe → l'herbe (*the grass*)

2. In the plural, the "s" of **les** or **des** is linked in pronunciation with the vowel that follows giving a "z" sound. The linking of a final consonant to the next word which starts with a vowel is called a **liaison**.

> les hôtels   des herbes
>   ∨   ∨
> *z sound*   *z sound*

NOTE: There are a few cases when the "h" is considered an "**h**" aspiré (an aspirate h). This *aspirate h* means that you must consider the word as if beginning with an invisible consonant. There are two important consequences:

1. In the singular, you do not drop the "e" at the end of **le** or the "a" of **la**; i.e. there is no elision.

> **le** héros   *the hero*
> **la** hâte   *the haste*

2. In the plural, there is no linking between the noun and the preceding word; i.e. there is no liaison.

> les héros   *the heros*

There are not many words that start with *an aspirate h*. They are usually identified in dictionaries with a dot under the "h" or with an asterisk in front of the word.

---

*An asterisk means that what follows is incorrect. It is included for the purpose of illustration.

14

<< What is the Possessive? >>

The term **possessive** means that one noun *possesses* another noun.

In English: You can show possession in one of two ways:

- by adding *apostrophe + s ('s)* to the possessor

    the lady*'s* handbag
    the tree*'s* branches
    the girl*s'* club
    the student*s'* teacher

- by adding *of the* before the possessor

    the handbag *of the* lady
    the branches *of the* tree
    the club *of the* girls
    the teacher *of the* students

In French: There is only one way to express possession, and that is by using *of the*. The apostrophe + s structure does not exist. When you want to express an apostrophe + s in French, be sure to change the structure.

the lady*'s* handbag	→	*the handbag of the lady* le sac **de la** dame
the tree*'s* branches	→	*the branches of the tree* les branches **de l'**arbre
the girl*s'* club	→	*the club of the girls* le club **des** filles
the student*s'* teacher	→	*the teacher of the students* le professeur **des** étudiants

For additional help with this structure in French see p.84.

<<   What is a Verb?   >>

A **verb** is a word that indicates an action, mental state or condition. The action can be physical, as in such verbs as *run, walk, hit, sit,* or mental, as in such verbs as *dream, think, believe,* and *hope.*

The verb is one of the most important words of a sentence, and you cannot express a complete thought (i.e., write a **complete sentence**) without a verb.

To help you learn to recognize verbs, here is a paragraph where the verbs are in italics:

> The three students *entered* the restaurant, *selected* a table, *hung* up their coats and *sat* down. They *looked* at the menu and *asked* the waitress what she *recommended*. She *advised* the daily special, beef stew. It *was* not expensive. They *chose* a bottle of red wine and *ordered* a salad. The service *was* slow, but the food *tasted* excellent. Good cooking, they *decided, takes* time. They *ordered* pastry for dessert and *finished* the meal with coffee.

A **transitive verb** is a verb that takes a direct object (see **What are Objects?** p.86). It is indicated by a (*v.t.*) in the dictionary.

> The boy *threw* the ball.   *to throw* — transitive verb
> /
> direct object

> She *quit* her job.   *to quit* — transitive verb
> /
> direct object

An **intransitive verb** is a verb that does not take a direct object. It is indicated by (*v.i.*) in the dictionary.

> Paul *is sleeping*.   *to sleep* — intransitive verb
> She *arrives* today.   *to arrive* — intransitive verb
> /
> adverb

Many verbs can be used *transitively* or *intransitively*, depending on whether they have a direct object in the sentence or not.

The students *speak* French.   *to speak* — transitive verb
/
direct object

Actions *speak* louder than words.
/   *to speak* — intransitive verb
adverb

In English: It is possible to change the meaning of a verb by placing little words (*prepositions* or *adverbs*) after them (Column A):

Column A	*Column B*
to look *for*	to search for
I am looking for a book.	
to look *after*	to take care of
I look after children.	
to look *out*	to beware of
Look out for lions.	
to look *into*	to investigate
He will look into it.	
to look *over*	to check
Look over the exam.	

In French: You cannot change the meaning of a verb by adding these little words. In French, you would have to use an entirely different verb in each of the above sentences.

When looking verbs up in the dictionary, be sure to look for the specific meaning of the verb (Column B).

<< What is an Infinitive? >>

An **infinitive** is a form of the verb. It is never used by itself as the main verb of a sentence, there must always be another verb with it (i.e., a verb that is conjugated—see **What is a Verb Conjugation?** p. 25).

In English: The infinitive form is introduced by the word *to*. When we want to speak about a verb in general, we usually give the infinitive form: *to love, to be, to think,* etc. It is the form we use to look up a word in the dictionary.

In a sentence, the infinitive form is always used with a conjugated verb.

To learn is exciting.
infinitive   main verb

It*'s* (*it is*) important *to be* on time.
main verb   infinitive

Bob and Mary *want to dance* together.
main verb   infinitive

It *has started to rain.*
auxiliary   main   infinitive

In French: The infinitive form is shown by the last two or three letters of the verb; there is no equivalent of *to*.

dé**tester**	*to detest*
fin**ir**	*to finish*
ven**dre**	*to sell*
rece**voir**	*to receive*

In a sentence, the infinitive form is always used for a verb that depends on another verb which is neither **avoir** nor **être**.

> *Bob and Mary want **to dance** together.*
> Bob et Marie *veulent* **danser** ensemble.
>   /
>   *infinitive*

> *Mary likes **to study** in her room.*
> Marie *aime* **étudier** dans sa chambre.
>   /
>   *infinitive*

> *Paul and Mary can **leave** if they wish.*
> Paul et Marie *peuvent* **partir** s'ils desirent.
>   /
>   *infinitive*

> *You should **telephone** today.*
> Vous *devriez* **téléphoner** aujourd'hui.
>   /
>   *infinitive*

Notice that in the last two examples you have no *to* in the English sentence to alert you that in French an infinitive must be used.

NOTES:

<<   What are Auxiliary Verbs?   >>

Some verbs can also be **auxiliary verbs** (also known as **helping verbs**); these auxiliary verbs help the main verb to express an action or make a statement.

Mary *is* a girl.	*is*	main verb
Paul *has* a headache.	*has*	main verb
They *go* to the movies.	*go*	main verb
They *have gone* to the movies.	*have*	auxiliary verb
	gone	main verb
His wife *has been gone* for two weeks.	*has*	auxiliary verb
	been	auxiliary verb
	gone	main verb

In English: There are many auxiliary verbs. They are used to indicate the tense of the main verb (*present, future, past*—see p. 31.)

Does he want to go out tonight?	Present
She *will* do her work tomorrow.	Future
John *used to* speak French.	Past

In French: There are only two auxiliary verbs: **avoir** (*to have*) and **être** (*to be*—see p. 38).

Le garçon **a mangé** la pomme.
      /   /
  auxiliary   *main verb*
  avoir

*The boy **has eaten** the apple.*

La fille **est allée** au cinéma.
      /   /
  auxiliary   *main verb*
  être

*The girl **has gone** to the movies.*

Since the other English auxiliary verbs do not exist as separate words in French, you cannot translate them as such. In French, the meaning conveyed by these auxiliary verbs is indicated by the last letters (*the ending*) of the main verb. You will find more on this subject under the different tenses.

<< What is a Subject? >>

In a sentence the person or thing that performs the action is called the **subject**. When you wish to find the subject of a sentence, always look for the verb first; then ask, "*who*?" or "*what*?" before the verb. The answer will be the subject.

John speaks French.

Who speaks French?   Answer: John

John is the subject.   (Singular subject)

Are John and Mary coming tonight?

Who is coming tonight?   Answer: John and Mary

John and Mary is the subject. (Plural subject)

Train yourself to always ask the question to find the subject. Never assume a word is the subject because it comes first in the sentence. Subjects can be in many different places of a sentence as you can see in the following examples in which the *subject* is in boldface and the *verb* italicised:

*Did **the game** start* on time?

After playing for two hours, ***John** became* exhausted.

Looking in the mirror *was* a little ***girl.***

Some sentences have more than one main verb; you have to find the subject of each verb.

> The *boys were doing* the cooking while *Mary was setting* the table.

>> *Boys* is the plural subject of *were doing.*

>> *Mary* is the singular subject of *was setting.*

In English and in French it is very important to find the subject of each verb and to make sure that the subject and verb agree; that is, you must choose the form of the verb which goes with the subject. (See **What is a Verb Conjugation? p. 25.**)

<< What is a Pronoun? >>

A **pronoun** is a word used in place of one or more nouns. It may stand, therefore, for a person, place, thing or idea.

For instance, instead of repeating the proper noun "Paul" in the following two sentences, we would use a pronoun in the second sentence:

> *Paul* likes to sing. *Paul* goes to practice every day.

> *Paul* likes to sing. *He* goes to practice every day.

A pronoun can only be used to refer to something (or someone) that has already been mentioned. The word that the pronoun replaces is called the **antecedent** of the pronoun.

In the example above, the pronoun "*he*" refers to the proper noun "*Paul .*" *Paul* is the antecedent of the pronoun *he.*

In English: There are different types of pronouns. They are studied in separate sections of this handbook. Below we will simply list the most important categories and refer you to the section where they are discussed in detail.

- **Personal pronouns** — These pronouns change in form in the different persons and according to the function they have in the sentence.

    - as *subject* (see p. 23)

        I go. *They* read. *He* runs.

    - as *direct object* (see p. 93)

        Paul loves *it*. Jane met *him*.

    - as *indirect* object (see p. 93)

        Jane gave the book *to her*. Speak to *them*.

    - as *disjunctives* (see p. 99)

        Who's there? *Me*. Who did it? *Us*.

- **Reflexive pronouns** — These pronouns are used with reflexive verbs (see p. 62).

    I cut *myself*. We washed *ourselves*.

- **Interrogative pronouns** — These pronouns are used in questions (see p. 103).

    Who is that? *What* do you want?

- **Demonstrative pronouns** — These pronouns are used to point out persons or things (see p. 114).

    This (one) is expensive. *That* (one) is cheap.

- **Possessive pronouns** — These pronouns are used to show possession (see p. 119).

    Whose book is that? *Mine*. *Yours* is on the table.

- **Relative pronouns** — These pronouns are used to introduce relative subordinate clauses (see p. 126).

    The man *who* came is very nice.
    Mary *whom* you met is the president of the
        company.

In French: Pronouns are identified in the same way as in English. The most important difference is that a pronoun agrees with the noun it replaces; that is, it must correspond in gender (and usually in number) with its antecedent.

<<   What is a Subject Pronoun?   >>

A **subject pronoun** is a pronoun that occurs as subject of the sentence.

Let us compare the personal subject pronouns of English and French.

English		French
I	1st person singular the person speaking	**je**
you	2nd person singular the person being spoken to	**tu**
he *she* *it*	3rd person singular the person or object being spoken about by the 1st and 2nd persons	**il** **elle**

we	1st person plural
	the person speaking
	plus others
	
	John and I like French.
	      \/
	    We
		nous

you	2nd person plural the persons being spoken to	**vous**
they	3rd person plural the persons or objects being spoken about by the 1st and 2nd persons	**ils** **elles**

In English: There is no difference between *you* in the singular and *you* in the plural. For example, if there were many people in a room and you asked out loud: "Are *you* coming with me?," the *you* could stand for one person or for many.

In French: There are two sets of pronouns for *you*:

- the *familiar form* — **tu** singular
  vous plural

  This form is used when you speak to children, family, friends, animals, or anyone with whom you are not on formal terms.

- the *formal form* — **vous** singular
  vous plural

  This form is used to address one or more persons you do not know very well.

  NOTE: When in doubt, always use the polite form, unless speaking to a child or animal.

NOTES:

<< What is a Verb Conjugation? >>

A **verb conjugation** is a list of the six possible forms of the verb, one form for each of the subject pronouns. Conjugations are always learned with pronouns.

In English: Verbs change very little. Let us look at the various forms the verb *to sing* takes in English when each of the six possible pronouns is the performer of the action.

1st per. sing.	*I sing* with the music.
2nd per. sing.	*You sing* with the music.
3rd per. sing.	{ *He sings* with the music.
	She sings with the music.
	It sings with the music.
1st per. pl.	*We sing* with the music.
2nd per. pl.	*You sing* with the music.
3rd per. pl.	*They sing* with the music.

Because English verbs change so little, you do not need "to conjugate verbs." It is much simpler to say that verbs take an "s" in the 3rd per. sing.

This is definitely not the case in French.

In French: Each verb usually has six different forms. It is necessary, therefore, to memorize a form of the verb for each of the six persons. Memorizing six forms for all verbs that exist would be an impossible and endless task. Fortunately, French verbs are divided into two overall categories:

1. **Regular verbs** — Verbs whose forms follow a regular pattern; only one sample must be memorized and the pattern can then be applied to all other verbs in the same group.

2. **Irregular verbs** — Verbs whose forms do not follow any regular pattern and must be memorized individually.

A. Let us look at the same verb *to sing* that we conjugated in English, paying special attention now to the personal subject pronoun:

1st per. sing.	**je** chante
2nd per. sing.	**tu** chantes
3rd per. sing.	⎰ **il** chante ⎱ **elle** chante
1st per. pl.	**nous** chantons
2nd per. pl.	**vous** chantez
3rd per. pl.	**ils** chantent **elles** chantent

You will have fewer problems knowing when to use the three singular persons (*I, you, he/she/it*—je, tu, il/elle), but you may confuse the three plural persons. Let us go over them.

- **1st person plural** — The *we* form of the verb is used whenever *I* (the speaker) is one of the *doers* of the action; that is, whenever the speaker is included in a plural or multiple subject (in italics):

  The students and I sing when the term is over.
  /
  In French: **nous** form

  Paul, Peter, Mary and I sing all day long.
  /
  In French: **nous** form

  In the two sentences above, the subject could be replaced by the pronoun *we*, so that in French you must use the **nous** form (1st per. pl.) of the verb.

- **2nd person plural** — The *you plural* form of the verb is used whenever:

  1. You are addressing more than one person to whom you say **tu**.

  Father: Peter, *come down* here.
  /
  In French: **tu** form

Mary, *turn off* the T.V.

/

In French: **tu** form

Get into the car both of you. I'm ready.

/

In French: **vous** form

2. You are addressing one or more persons formally.

Mrs. Smith, *are* you ready?

/

In French: **vous** form

Mr. and Mrs. Smith, *are* you ready?

/

In French: **vous** form

- **3rd person plural** — The *they* form of the verb is used whenever you are speaking about a plural or multiple subject which <u>does not</u> include either the speaker or the person being spoken to (in italics):

The boys sing when the term is over.

/

In French: **ils** form

Paul, Peter, and Henry sing all day long.

/

In French: **ils** form

(Compare with: *Paul, Peter, Henry and I sing* ...)

/

In French: **nous** form

The glasses and the cokes are on the counter.

/

In French: **ils** form

In the three sentences above, the subject could be replaced by *they*, so that in French you must use the 3rd person plural of the verb.

B. Let us now look at the same verb *to sing*, paying special attention to the verb form.

je	chant**e**
tu	chant**es**
il	chant**e**
elle	chant**e**
nous	chant**ons**
vous	chant**ez**
ils	chant**ent**
elles	chant**ent**

One speaks of a French verb as being composed of two parts:

1. the *stem* (**la racine,** literally "the root") which undergoes only minor changes, if any, in a conjugation of a regular verb.

2. the *ending* (**la terminaison**) which changes for each person in the conjugation of regular and irregular verbs.

French verbs are divided into groups according to the infinitive ending. Unlike English where the infinitive is the word *to* plus the verb, in French the infinitive form is a special ending attached to the stem (see p. 17). The four most common endings are:

-er	-ir	-re	-oir
(1st group)	(2nd group)	(3rd group)	(4th group)

You will only have to memorize one sample verb for each group of regular verbs. As an example, let's look more closely at samples of regular verbs of the 1st group, or 1st conjugation.

- All have an infinitive ending in **-er.**

    chant**er**   parl**er**   aim**er**

- All add the same endings to their stem.

je	chante	parle	aime
tu	chantes	parles	aimes
il	chante	parle	aime
elle	chante	parle	aime
nous	chantons	parlons	aimons
vous	chantez	parlez	aimez
ils	chantent	parlent	aiment
elles	chantent	parlent	aiment

When memorizing the conjugation of regular verbs of any group, you must:

1. Separate the stem from the ending.

2. Add the ending that agrees with your subject.

A special word must be said about the first conjugation. Although, you can easily <u>see</u> the difference between the various verb forms when they are written, you will have to learn to <u>hear</u> the difference among the various verb forms. You must listen for certain clues:

1. The *subject pronoun*

Since the verb endings in *chante, chantes, chante* and *chantent* are all pronounced the same, you must listen for the subject pronoun.

je chante
tu chantes
il chante/**ils** chantent
elle chante/**elles** chantent

2. The *context*

Only the context will help you to distinguish between the 3rd person singular and plural when the verb begins with a consonant. You must listen for clues in the previous sentence:

Paul chante. **Il** danse aussi.

Paul et Robert chantent. **Ils** dansent aussi.

‾‾‾‾‾‾‾‾‾‾‾‾‾
La musicienne chante. Elle danse aussi.

‾‾‾‾‾‾‾‾‾‾‾‾‾
Les musiciennes chantent. Elles dansent aussi.

3. The *liaison*

Although the subject pronouns of the 3rd person singular and plural (**il, ils** and **elle, elles**) are pronounced the same, you can <u>hear</u> the difference between the singular and the plural when the verb begins with a vowel. Listen for the "z" sound of the linking (*liaison*) between the subject pronoun and the verb:

Il adore la musique.　　Ils adorent la musique.
　　∨　　　　　　　　　　　∨
no z sound　　　　　　*z sound*
indicates singular　　*indicates plural*

Elle écoute le disque.　Elles écoutent le disque.
　　∨　　　　　　　　　　　∨
no z sound　　　　　　*z sound*
indicates singular　　*indicates plural*

<<　What is a Mood?　>>

The many forms a verb can take are divided into different **moods**. As a beginning student of French, all you have to know are the names of the moods so that you will understand what your French grammar book is referring to. You will learn when to use the various moods as you learn verbs and their tenses.

In English: Verbs can be in one of three moods:

1. The **indicative** mood — This is the most common mood and most of the verb forms that you use when you speak are in the indicative mood. (See **What is the Present Tense?** p. 32; **What is the Past Tense?** p. 45; **What is the Future Tense?** p. 50.)

2. The **imperative** mood (see p. 33).

3. The **subjunctive** mood (see p. 61).

In French: The French language identifies four moods, instead of the English three. In addition to the three moods listed above, there is the **conditional** mood (see p. 55). As in English, the indicative mood is the most common mood and most of the tenses you will learn belong to the indicative mood.

<<   What is Meant by Tense?   >>

The word **tense** comes from the French word "temps" which means *time*. The tense, then, means the time when the action of the verb takes place (at the *present* time, in the *past*, or in the *future* for example).

I *am eating.*	Present
I *ate.*	Past
I *will eat.*	Future

As you can see in the above examples, just by putting the verb in a different tense and without giving any additional information (such as "I am eating *now*," "I ate *yesterday*," "I will eat *tomorrow*"), you can indicate when the action of the verb takes place.

<< What is the Present Tense? >>

The **present tense** indicates that the action is going on at the present time. It can be:

- at the time the speaker is speaking (I *see* you.)
- a habitual action (He *smokes* when he *is* nervous.)
- a general truth (The sun *shines* every day.)

In English: There are three forms of the verb which, although they have a slightly different meaning, all indicate the present tense.

> Mary *studies* in the library.   Present
>
> Mary *is studying* in the library.   Present progressive
>
> Mary *does study* in the library.   Present emphatic

In French: There is only one verb form to indicate the present tense. It is indicated by the ending of the verb, without any helping verb such as *is* and *does*. It is very important, therefore, not to translate these helping verbs used in English. Simply put the main verb in the present.

> *Mary **studies** in the library.*
> étudie

> *Mary **is studying** in the library.*
> étudie

> *Mary **does study** in the library.*
> étudie

<< What is the Imperative? >>

The **imperative** is the command form of a verb. It is used to give someone an order.

In English: There are two verb forms:

you	2nd person (same for singular and plural)
Let's	1st person plural

The *present tense* (not the present progressive) is used and the subject pronoun is dropped.

Statement	→		→	Command
(present progressive)	→	(present)	→	(imperative)
You are answering the phone.		*You answer* the phone.		*Answer* the phone.
We are going out.		*We go out.*		*Let's go out.*

In French: There are three verb forms:

you	2nd person singular	**tu** form
Let's	1st person plural	**nous** form
you	2nd person plural	**vous** form

The *present tense* of the verb is used and the subject pronoun is dropped:

Statement	→	Command
(present tense)		(imperative)
Tu **réponds** au téléphone.	→	**Réponds** au téléphone.
Nous **sortons** maintenant.		**Sortons** maintenant.
Vous **répondez** au téléphone.		**Répondez** au téléphone.

NOTE: 1. Make sure that you drop the final -s of the **tu** form in the present tense of verbs of the first conjugation (**-er** verbs) when you use that form in the imperative.

Present	→	Imperative
Tu chantes maintenant.		**Chante** maintenant.
You are singing now.		*Sing now.*

2. Do not try to translate the *let's* of the 1st person plural; ignore it.

Chantons maintenant.   *Let's sing now.*

NOTES:

<< What are Declarative and Interrogative Sentences? >>

Sentences are classified according to their purpose. A **declarative sentence** is a sentence that makes a statement.

Columbus discovered America in 1492.

An **interrogative sentence** is a sentence that asks a question.

When did Columbus discover America?

In written language, an interrogative sentence always has a question mark at the end.

In English: To change a statement (S) into a question (Q), you sometimes need the helping verb (auxiliary) *do/does/did* before the subject. This auxiliary verb serves to alert you that what follows is a question.

S: Paul and Mary go out together.
Q: *Do* Paul and Mary go out together?

S: Mark likes pretty girls.
Q: *Does* Mark like pretty girls?

S: Frank and June just got married.
Q: *Did* Frank and June just get married?

Another way to make a question is to switch the verb and the subject around, placing the verb before the subject. This reversing of the normal "subject + verb" order is called **inversion.**

S: *They are* home this evening.
Q: *Are they* home this evening?

In French: All statements can be changed into a question by using one of these two interrogative forms:

1. Adding the expression **Est-ce que** before the statement which is left intact. Like *do/does/did*, **est-ce que** serves to alert you that what follows is a question.

S: Paul et Marie sortent ensemble.
Q: **Est-ce que** Paul et Marie sortent ensemble?
(Do   Paul and Mary go out together?)

S: Marc aime les jolies filles.
Q: **Est-ce que** Marc aime les jolies filles?
(Does   Mark like pretty girls?)

S: Pierre et Marie sont allés en France en juin.
Q: **Est-ce que** Pierre et Marie sont allés en France en juin?
(Did   Peter and Mary go to France in June?)

NOTE: Make sure that you ignore *do/does/did* when you are using French. French has no such auxiliary verbs.

2. When using the **inversion form**, that is, the verb <u>followed</u> by the subject, you will first have to look for the subject and see if it is a noun or a pronoun.

• If the subject is a pronoun, simply invert the verb and the pronoun subject:

S: **Vous êtes** à la maison ce soir.
You are home   this evening.

Q: **Etes-vous** à la maison ce soir?
Are you home   this evening.

• If the subject is a noun, follow these steps in order:

1. Give the noun (the subject).
2. Give the verb and, when writing, a hyphen.
3. Give the subject pronoun which corresponds to the subject (see p. 23 & 26-27).

S: *Paul is home this evening.*
Q:**Paul is he home this evening?*

S: Paul est à la maison ce soir.
Q: **Paul** est-**il** à la maison ce soir?

S: *Paul and Helen are home this evening.*
Q:*Paul and Helen are they home this evening?*

S: Paul et Hélène sont à la maison ce soir.
Q: Paul et Hélène sont-ils à la maison ce soir?

When a verb has more than one subject (in this case *Paul* and *Helen*) and one of the subjects is masculine (*Paul*), the entire subject is considered as being masculine. Therefore, *Paul* and *Helen* are considered as masculine plural and correspond to the pronoun **ils.**

S: *The watch and the key are on the table.*
Q:*The watch and the key are they on the table?*

S: La montre et la clé sont sur la table.
Q: La montre et la clé sont-elles sur la table?

Since both subjects (*la montre* and *la clé*) are feminine, the subject is considered feminine plural. Therefore, the pronoun used is **elles.**

NOTE: These are the two basic forms for asking a question. Use only one form or the other: either use the **est-ce que** form with no inversion of the verb and subject or use the inversion.

*An asterisk before a sentence means the sentence is ungrammatical. The purpose of including such a sentence is to compare it to the French one.

<< What is the Importance of the Verbs >>
Avoir (to have) and Être (to be)?

The verbs *to have* and *to be* are irregular verbs in French that have to be memorized. They are important verbs because they serve both as main verbs and auxiliary verbs:

	avoir	être
Main verb:	Marie **a** trois frères. *Mary **has** three brothers.*	Jean **est** malade. *John **is** sick.*
Auxiliary:	Marie **a** pris son livre. *Marie **has** taken her book.*	Jean **est** parti. *John **is** gone.*

The use of **avoir** and **être** as auxiliaries is discussed in detail on p. 46.

Concerning the spoken language, it is important to hear and pronounce correctly the difference between the third person plural of **avoir** and **être**.

ils ont **(avoir)**   ils sont **(être)**
z sound   *s sound*

It might help you to remember that the two "ss" one next to the other in "ils sont" account for the "s" sound.

The use of *to have* and *to be* is somewhat different in French than in English, and in the course of your study of French you will learn how to use each verb. Here are a few examples of the most common differences:

1. Many French expressions use the verb **avoir** (to have) where the English equivalent uses the verb *to be*.

I am hungry.	*to be*
J'ai faim.	**avoir**

I am 21 years old.	*to be*
J'ai 21 ans.	**avoir**

When an expression cannot be translated directly word for word into French, it is called an **idomatic expression** (or an **idiom**). These expressions will have to be memorized.

2. The French expression **il y a** corresponds to *there is, there are* when you are describing the location of something. It is **invariable**; that is, it never changes in form. You must learn how to use this very common expression and not to use the 3rd person of **être** (**est** — *is*, or **sont** — *are*) when you shouldn't.

To avoid using the wrong form, see if you can replace the *is* or *are* of the English sentence, with *there is* or *there are*. If you can, use **il y a**. If you cannot, use **est** or **sont** as the case may be.

On the table *is* a book.　→　On the table *there is* a
　　　/　　　　　　　　　　　book.
　In French: **il y a**

The book *is* on the table.　→　*The book *there is* on
　　　/　　　　　　　　　　　the table.
　In French: **est**

In the room *are* chairs and tables.　→　In the room *there are*
　　　/　　　　　　　　　　　chairs and tables.
　In French: **il y a**

The chairs and tables *are* in the room. → *The chairs and tables
　　　/　　　　　　　　　　　*there are* in the room.
　　　In French: **sont**

---

*An asterisk before a sentence means the sentence is ungrammatical. The purpose of including such a sentence is to compare it to the French one.

3. The French expression **voilà** corresponds to *there is, there are,* with the stress on *there,* when pointing out objects.

> *There is* the book you are looking for.
>
> In French: **voilà**

> *There are* my friends. Do you see them?
>
> In French: **voilà**

Do not confuse **voilà** and **il y a.** Make sure that you use **il y a** when giving a description, an explanation or the location of something.

> *There is* a book on the shelf in the bedroom.
>
> In French: **il y a**

> *There are* many ski resorts in the Alps.
>
> In French: **il y a**

<< What is a Participle? >>

A **participle** has two functions: 1. It is a form of the verb that is used in combination with an auxiliary verb to indicate certain tenses. 2. It may be used as an adjective or modifier to describe something.

> I *was writing* a letter.
>
> auxiliary   participle

> The *broken* vase was on the floor.
>
> participle describing *vase*

There are two types of participles: the **present participle** and the **past participle.** As you will learn in your study of French, participles are not used in the same way in the two languages.

A. The **present participle**

In English: The present participle is easy to recognize because it is the **-ing** form of the verb: *working, studying, dancing, playing,* etc.

The present participle is used:

- as the main verb in certain tenses

    She is *singing.*
    They were *dancing.*

- as an adjective

    This is an *amazing* discovery.
    /
    describes the noun *discovery*

    She read an *interesting* book.
    /
    describes the noun *book*

- as a modifier

    Turning the corner, Tony ran into a tree.

    The entire phrase *turning the corner* modifies or describes *Tony.*

    Look at the cat *climbing* the tree.

    Climbing the tree modifies the noun *cat.*

In French: The present participle is formed by adding **-ant** to the stem of the **nous** form of the present tense.

Present tense	*Present participle*
chant**ons**	chant**ant**
finiss**ons**	finiss**ant**
répond**ons**	répond**ant**
recev**ons**	recev**ant**

The present participle is not used in the same way in French as in English, and it is usually introduced at a more advanced level of French.

As a beginner, you must keep in mind that the equivalent of common English tenses formed with an *auxiliary + present participle* *(she is singing, they are dancing)* <u>do not</u> use participles in French. These English constructions correspond to a French tense.

*She **is singing**.*	Elle **chante**.
/	/
present	présent

*They **were dancing**.*	Ils **dansaient**.
/	/
past progressive	imparfait

*He **will be writing**.*	Il écrira.
/	/
future	futur

As you can see in the examples above, the tense of the auxiliary verb of the English construction corresponds to the tense of the French verb. (For more details, look under the different French tenses.)

Here are some pointers to help you avoid making mistakes in using the present participle:

1. In French the present participle is used much less frequently than in English.

2. Never assume that an English word ending with *-ing* is translated by its French counterpart ending in -ant. Consult your French grammar book for rules regarding the use of the present participle.

B. The **past participle**

In English: It is formed in several ways. You can always find it by remembering the form of the verb you would use following *I have.*

> I have *spoken.*
>
> I have *written.*
>
> I have *walked.*

The past participle is used:

- as an adjective

  > Is the *written* word more important
  > than the *spoken* word?
  >
  > > *Written* describes the noun *word.*
  > > *Spoken* describes the noun *word.*

- as a verb form in combination with the auxiliary verb have

  > I *have written* all that I have to say.
  >
  > He *hasn't spoken* to me since our quarrel.

In French: A verb can have a **regular past participle**, that is a past participle formed according to a regular pattern:

Infinitive ending		Past participle ending	
-er	(chanter)	-é	(chanté)
-ir	(finir)	-i	(fini)
-re	(répondre)	-u	(répondu)
-oir	(vouloir)	-u	(voulu)

or an **irregular past participle** that you will have to memorize just as you memorize vocabulary:

Infinitive	Past participle
être	été
avoir	eu
écrire	écrit
comprendre	compris

44

As in English, the past participle can be used as an adjective or as a verb form.

- When the past participle is used as an adjective, it must agree with the noun it modifies in gender and in number.

*The **spoken** language*

> *Spoken* modifies the noun *language.*
>
> Since the French word for *language* is feminine singular **(la langue)**, the word for *spoken* in French is feminine singular, shown by the addition of an **e**.

La langue **parlée**

*The **written** words*

> *Written* modifies the noun *words.*
>
> Since the French word for *words* is masculine plural **(les mots)**, the word for *written* in French is masculine plural, shown by the addition of an **s**.

Les mots **écrits**

- The most important use of the past participle in French is as a verb form in combination with an auxiliary verb to indicate the past tense (see **What is the Past Tense?**).

NOTES:

<< What is the Past Tense? >>

The **past tense** is used to express an action that occurred in the past.

In English: There are several verb forms that indicate that the action took place in the past.

I worked	Simple past
I was working	Past progressive
I used to work	With helping verb *used to*
I did work	Past emphatic
I have worked	Present perfect

In French: There are only two verb forms to indicate the past tense **l'imparfait** *(the imperfect)* and **le passé composé** *(the past indefinite)*.

The **imparfait** is formed by attaching certain endings to the stem of the verb. The conjugation is so regular that there is no need to add to what is in your French grammar book.

The **passé composé** is composed of an auxiliary verb conjugated in the present **+ *the past participle*.** As in English, the past participle is not conjugated (i.e., it does not change form from one person to another: *I* have *written, He* has *written*).

According to the auxiliary verb used (see below), the past participle follows certain rules of agreement which your French grammar book surely outlines. Since the past participle conjugated with **être** agrees with the subject, go over the section **What is a Subject?** p. 20. Past participles conjugated with **avoir** agree with the direct object if it comes before the verb. You should go over the section **What are Objects?** p. 86.

Unlike English where the past participle can be used with several auxiliary verbs, the past participle in French can only be used with one of two French auxiliary verbs, **avoir** or **être**.

je **suis** allé *(went;* *have gone)*	j'**ai** mangé *(ate;* *have eaten)*
tu **es** allé	tu **as** mangé

Your problem will be determining whether a verb takes **avoir** or **être** as the auxiliary. Since most verbs take **avoir**, it will be easier for you to memorize only the verbs conjugated with **être**. You can assume that all the other verbs are conjugated with **avoir**. There are approximately twelve basic verbs, sometimes referred to as "verbs of motion," that are conjugated with **être**. "Verbs of motion," is not really an accurate description of these verbs since some of them, such as **rester** *(to stay, to remain)*, do not imply motion. You will find these verbs easy to memorize in pairs, since you can group them by "opposites":

aller	*to go*	venir	*to come*
entrer	*to come in*	sortir	*to go out*
arriver	*to arrive*	partir	*to leave*
monter	*to climb*	descendre	*to go down*
rester	*to remain*	tomber	*to fall*
naitre	*to be born*	mourir	*to die*

The verbs derived from the above verbs are also conjugated with **être**: **rentrer**, **revenir**, **devenir**, among others.

In choosing the correct tense in French between the **imparfait** and the **passé composé**, the English verb form will rarely tell you which tense the French verb should be in. To select the right tense you will have to rely on the rules in your French grammar book.

In brief, the **imparfait** and the **passé composé** take place at the same time in the past. However when the duration of one action is compared to the duration of another action in the same sentence or story, the **imparfait** is used for the longer or more continuous of the two actions.

> *I was reading* when he *came in.*
>   /   /
> imparfait   passé composé

Both actions are taking place at the same time, but the action of *reading* is continuous and the *coming in* just took an instant.

You might also note that there are two English verb forms that indicate when the **imparfait** should be used.

- If the English verb form includes, or could include, the helping verb ***used to.***

> *When I was a child* { *I used to sing.*
>   { *I sang.*

I was expresses the idea of a continuous duration; *I sang* has the same meaning as *I used to sing.* Therefore, in French, you use the **imparfait** for both verbs.

> Quand j'**étais** enfant, je **chantais.**

- If the English verb form is in the past progressive tense, as *was laughing, were running.*

> *I was working all day long.*

> Je **travaillais** toute la journée.

You should practice choosing the correct French past tense with English texts, without translating them. Pick out the verbs in the past tense and indicate for each one if you would put it in the **imparfait** or in the **passé composé.** Remember that selecting one of these two possible past tenses gives the verb a slightly different meaning. Sometimes both tenses are possible, but usually one of the two is more logical.

<< What is the Past Perfect (<u>Plus-Que-Parfait</u>)? >>

The **past perfect** tense is used to express an action completed in the past <u>before</u> some other past action or event.

In English: It is formed with the auxiliary *had* (which is the past tense of the verb *to have*) *+ the past participle.*

The past perfect is used when two actions happened at different times in the past and you want to make it clear which of the actions preceded the other.

She suddenly *remembered* that she *had not eaten* yet.

/ /

past tense   past perfect

(1)   (2)

Both action (1) and action (2) occurred in the past, but action (2) preceded action (1). Therefore, action (2) is in the past perfect.

Don't forget that verb tenses indicate the time that an action occurred. Therefore, when verbs in the same sentence are in the **imparfait**, the action took place at the same time. In order to show that they took place at different times, different tenses must be used. Look at the following examples:

- The car *was sliding* because it *was raining.*

/ /

past progressive   past progressive

(1)   (2)

Action (1) and action (2) took place at the same time.

- The car *was sliding* because it *had rained.*

/ /

past progressive   past perfect

(1)   (2)

Action (2) took place before action (1).

In French: The French term for past perfect is **plus-que-parfait**. It is used to make clear that an action took place <u>before</u> an action in the **passé composé** or the **imparfait**. It is formed by putting the auxiliary verb **avoir** or **être** in the **imparfait** *+ the past participle.* The rules of agreement of the past participle are the same as for the **passé composé** (see p.45).

Look at this line showing the relationship of tenses:

Verb tense:	**Plus-que-parfait**	**Passé composé Imparfait**	**Présent**	**Futur**
	D	C	A	B
Time action takes place:	*before "C"*	*before "A"*	*now*	*after "A"*

When we write the above two sentences in French, you will see that in French and in English the same relationship exists between the time the action took place.

- *The car **was sliding** because it **was raining**.*

  La voiture **dérapait** parce qu'il **pleuvait**.
  imparfait   imparfait
  "C"   "C"

Two actions in the **imparfait** show that they took place at the same time in the past.

- *The car **was sliding** because it **had rained**.*

  La voiture **dérapait** parce qu'il **avait plu**.
  imparfait   plus-que-parfait
  "C"   "D"

The action in the **plus-que-parfait** (point D) occurred before the action in the **imparfait** (point C).

50

You cannot always rely on English to determine when to use the past perfect. English usage permits the use of the simple past in many cases to describe an action that preceded another, if it is clear which action came first.

*The teacher **wanted** to know who **saw** the student.*
/   /
simple past   *simple past*

*The teacher **wanted** to know who **had seen** the student.*
/   /
simple past   *past perfect*

Although the two sentences above mean the same thing and are correct English, only the verb sequence of the second sentence would be correct in French.

Le professeur **voulait** savoir qui **avait vu** l'étudiant.
/   /
imparfait   plus-que-parfait
"C"   "D"

The verb in the past perfect (point D) stresses that the action was completed before the action of "wanting to know" (point C). In French grammar, agreement of tenses is more strict than in English.

<< What is the Future Tense? >>

The **future tense** indicates that an action will take place sometime in the future.

In English: It is formed by means of the auxiliary *will* or *shall + the main verb.*

Paul and Mary *will do* their homework tomorrow.

I *shall go out* tonight.

In French: You do not need an auxiliary to show that the action will take place in the future. Future time is indicated by attaching different endings for each person to:

- the infinitive form of regular verbs

    aimer-
    finir-
    vendr-   *(The final "e" is dropped.)*

- special irregular future verb stems

    ir-   (aller)
    viendr-   (venir)
    aur-   (avoir)
    ser-   (être)

You will notice that whatever the infinitive or stem, regular or irregular, the sound of the letter "r" is always heard before the future ending.

In English and in French, the fact that an action will occur sometime in the future can also be expressed without using the future tense.

In English: You can use the verb *to go in the present progressive + the infinitive.* Thus,

    I *am going* to sing.
       /   /
    present progressive   infinitive
    of *to go*

means the same thing as

    I *shall* sing.
        /
    future of *to sing*

In French; You can likewise use the verb **aller** *(to go) in the present + the infinitive.* Thus,

Je **vais** *chanter.*
/   /
present   infinitive

means the same thing as

Je **chanterai.**
/
future of **chanter**

Other examples:

I shall buy a book.	→	*I am going to buy a book.*
/ future of *to buy*		/ present progressive of *to go* + infinitive
J'achèterai un livre.	→	Je **vais** acheter un livre.
/ *future of* **acheter**		/ *present of* **aller** + *infinitive*

In conversational French, **aller** + *infinitive* often replaces the future tense.

<<   **What is the Future Perfect (Futur Antérieur)?**   >>

The **future perfect** tense is used to express an action which will be completed in the future <u>before</u> some other specific action or event occurs in the future. It is only used when two actions will happen at different times in the future and you want to stress which one of the actions will come first.

In English: The **future perfect** is formed with the auxiliaries *will have* or *shall have* + *the past participle.*

- By the time school opens, I *will have finished.*

  |_____| /
  specific event in the future   future perfect
              (1)   (2)

  Both action (2) and event (1) will occur at some future time, but action (2) will be completed before event (1) takes place. Therefore, action (2) is in the future perfect tense.

- By the time she arrives, I *will have left.*

  |_____| /
  specific event in the future   future perfect
              (1)   (2)

  Action (2) will be completed before event (1) takes place. Therefore, action (2) is in the future perfect tense.

In French: The **futur antérieur** is formed by using the auxiliary of the verb **avoir** or **être** *in the future tense + the past participle* of the main verb.

- *I'll have eaten   before his arrival.*

  J'aurai mangé   avant son arrivée.
       / |_____|
  futur antérieur   *specific event in the future*
       (2)   (1)

  Action (2) will be completed before event (1) takes place. Therefore, action (2) is in the **futur antérieur.**

- *I'll be gone   before 10 p.m.*

  Je **serai parti**   avant 10 heures du soir.
       / |_____|
  futur antérieur   *specific event in the future*
       (2)   (1)

  Action (2) will be completed before event (1) takes place. Therefore, action (2) is in the **futur antérieur.**

Observe this time line showing the relationship of future tenses:

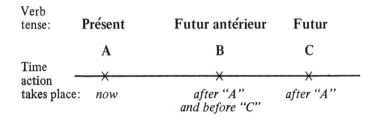

Verb
tense: **Présent**   **Futur antérieur**   **Futur**

         A   **B**   **C**

Time
action
takes place: *now*   *after "A"*   *after "A"*
                        and before "C"

To use "B" (**futur antérieur**) you have to have "C" (**futur**) with which to contrast it. You do not need "A" in the same sentence. Also, "C" must represent a specific action or event in the future; it can be a verb phrase ("before *he arrives*") or a noun phrase ("before his *arrival*").

Compare these sentences:

- *This evening, the children will eat, go to bed, and then we will go out.*

  Ce soir, les enfants **mangeront** et **iront** au lit, et ensuite nous **sortirons.**

  futur "C" (sortirons), futur "C" (mangeront), futur "C" (iront)

All the verbs are in the future tense (point "C" on the time line) because you are listing a series of things you are going to do in the future, "this evening."

- *This evening, we will go out after the children have eaten and gone to bed.*

  Ce soir, nous **sortirons** après que les enfants **auront**

  futur "C" (sortirons), futur (auront)

  mangé et se **seront couchés.**

  antérieur "B" (mangé), futur antérieur "B" (seront couchés)

In French, the future perfect is required even though it is not used in English. Both the verbs in the future perfect (point "B") stress that those actions will be accomplished before the action of "going out" (point "C"). In French grammar, agreement of tenses is more strict than in English.

<< What is the Conditional? >>

The **conditional** is an important French mood (**le conditionnel**); modern English grammar books, however, do not include it. The use of the French **conditionnel** and what we will call for our purposes the English "conditional" are sufficiently similar to justify a comparison.

NOTE: The use of the conditional both in English and in French does not necessarily mean that the sentence implies a "condition."

In English: The "conditional" is a form of the verb composed of the auxiliary *would + the "dictionary form" of the main verb.*[1] This is called the **present conditional**.

> I said that I *would come* tomorrow.
>
> If she had the money, she *would call* him.
>
> I *would like* some ketchup, please.

NOTE: The auxiliary *would* in English has several meanings. It does not correspond to the conditional when it stands for *used to*, as in "She *would talk* while he painted." In this sentence, the verb means *used to* and requires the **imparfait** in French.

---

[1] The form under which a verb is listed in a dictionary.

The **past conditional** is composed of the auxiliary *would have + the past participle of the main verb.*

He *would have spoken*, if he had known the truth.

If she had had the time, she *would have written* to him.

I *would have eaten*, if I had been hungry.

The "conditional" is used in the following ways:

- in the main clause of a **hypothetical** (imaginary) statement

    If I were rich, I *would buy* a Cadillac.

"I would buy a Cadillac" is called the **main clause**, or **result clause.** It is a **clause** because it is composed of a group of words containing a subject *(I)* and a verb *(would buy)* and is used as part of a sentence. It is the **main clause** because it expresses a complete thought and can stand by itself as a complete sentence.

"If I were rich" is called the **subordinate clause**, or **"if" clause.** Although it contains a subject *(I)* and a verb *(were)*, it does not express a complete thought and can not stand alone.

- in the subordinate clause to express a **future in the past** (This means that the main clause must be in the past.)

    He said that he *would come.*
       (1)   (2)

Action (2) of the subordinate clause takes place after action (1). Therefore, action (2) is a future in the past and takes the conditional.

If the main clause is in the present, then the *future tense* is used to express a future action.

    He *says* that he *will come.*
      present   future

- as a polite form with "like"

  I *would like* to eat.

  This is more "polite" than "I *want* to eat."

In French: You do not need an auxiliary to show the conditional; the **conditionnel présent** is indicated by attaching the **imparfait** endings to:

- the infinitive form of regular verbs

      aimer-
      finir-
      vendr-   *(The final "e" is dropped.)*

- the special irregular future verb stems (see p. 51)

      ir-   (aller)
      viendr-   (venir)
      aur-   (avoir)
      ser-   (être)

In spoken language, there is no way to distinguish between the 1st person singular of the conditional and the future.

      J'irai.   J'irais.
        /   /
      futur   conditionnel

The **conditionnel passé** is formed by putting the auxiliary of the verb **avoir** or **être** in the **conditionnel présent** + *the past participle of the main verb.*

   He would have spoken, if he had known the truth.
          /   /
    past conditional   *past perfect*

   Il **aurait parlé**, s'il **avait su** la vérité.
        /   /
   conditionnel passé   plus-que-parfait

Let us study more examples of English conditionals, so that you learn to recognize them and use the French conditional.

1. Sequence of tenses in **hypothetical statements**: First, how do you recognize a hypothetical statement? It is always made up of two clauses:

   a) the *"if" clause*; that is, the clause that starts with *"if"* (**si** in French).

   b) the *"result clause"*; that is, the main clause.

The tense sequence is the same in English and in French. In case you have problems recognizing tenses, just apply these three simple rules:

- *"if" clause* – present tense = *"result clause"* future

  If he **comes**,   **I'll be** happy.
  /   /
  present   future

  S'il **vient**,   je **serai** contente.
  /   /
  présent   futur

- *"if" clause* – $\begin{cases} \text{past} \\ \textbf{imparfait} \end{cases}$ = *"result clause"* conditional

  If he **came**,   I **would (I'd) be** happy.
  /   /
  past   conditional

  S'il **venait**,   je **serais** content.
  /   /
  imparfait   conditionnel

- *"if" clause* – past perfect = *"result clause"* past conditional

  If he **had come**,   I **would have been** happy.
  /   /
  past perfect   past conditional

S'il était venu, **j'aurais été** contente.
/ /
plus-que-parfait conditionnel passé

In English and in French the *"if" clause* can come either at the beginning of the sentence before the main clause, or at the end of the sentence. Observe in the following examples how the tense used is attached to the type of clause, not to the clause order.

- *I'll be happy, if he comes.*
/ /
future   *present*

Je **serai** heureuse, s'il **vient.**
/ /
futur   présent

If he comes, I'll be happy.
/ /
present *future*

S'il **vient,** je **serai** heureuse.
/ /
présent futur

- *I'd be happy, if he came.*
/ /
conditional   *past*

Je **serais** heureuse, s'il **venait.**
/ /
conditionnel   imparfait

If he came, I'd be happy.
/ /
past *conditional*

S'il **venait,** je **serais** heureuse.
/ /
imparfait conditionnel

2. The conditional in the subordinate clause to express a **future in the past** (see p. 56).

Identify the English tense and use the French equivalent.

- *I knew (that) it would rain this evening.*
  /   /
  past   *present conditional*

  Je **savais** qu'il **pleuvrait** ce soir.
  /   /
  imparfait   conditionnel présent

- *The girl thought (that) he would write a letter.*
  /   /
  past   *present conditional*

  La fille **croyait** qu'il **écrirait** une lettre.
  /   /
  imparfait   conditionnel présent

3. The conditional as a **polite form** with "like"

- *I would like a sandwich.*   (instead of: I *want* a
  /   sandwich.)
  conditional

  Je **voudrais** un sandwich.
  /
  conditionnel présent

- *I would like to go out this evening.*   (instead of: I *want*
  /   /   to go out this
  conditional   *infinitive*   evening.)

  J'**aimerais** sortir ce soir.
  /   \
  conditionnel   infinitif
  présent

<< What is the Subjunctive? >>

The **subjunctive** mood exists in English, but it is used only in a few cases. It occurs in:

- contrary-to-fact statements

  If I *were* you, I would go on vacation. (But I'm not you.)

  She talked as though she *were* my boss. (But she isn't my boss.)

- statements expressing a wish that is not possible

  I wish it *were* not true.   (But it is true.)

  I wish she *were* my teacher. (But she isn't my teacher.)

- the *that* clause following verbs of asking, demanding and recommending

  I recommend that he *take* the course. (Instead of "takes")

  I demanded that she *come* to see me. (Instead of "comes")

These are just a few examples to show you that English has the subjunctive form too. In French, the subjunctive is used very frequently, but unfortunately, English usage will not help you here. In the sentences above, only the second and third examples above would take the subjunctive in French. Therefore, we refer you to the explanations and examples of the subjunctive in your French grammar book. We can only encourage you to memorize the verbs, expressions and clauses which require the subjunctive form of the verb.

62

<< What is a Reflexive Verb? >>

A **reflexive verb** is a verb conjugated with a personal pronoun used "to reflect" the action of the verb on the performer, that is the subject of the sentence. The result is that the subject of the sentence and the object are the same person.

In English: The personal pronouns *-self* or *-selves* (*myself, yourself,* etc.) are used with reflexive verbs.

Here are the English reflexive pronouns:

myself	ourselves
yourself	yourselves
himself	themselves
herself	
itself	

Observe their usage in the following examples:

I cut *myself.*

You dried *yourself* with a towel.

Paul and Mary blamed *themselves* for the accident.

In French: The reflexive pronouns are:

me	*myself*
te	*yourself*
se	*himself, herself, itself*
nous	*ourselves*
vous	*yourselves*
se	*themselves*

Since the reflexive pronoun reflects the action of the verb on the performer, the reflexive pronoun will change as the subject of the verb changes. You will have to memorize the conjugation of reflexive verbs with the subject pronoun <u>and</u> the reflexive pronoun. For example, let's took at the verb **se laver** *(to wash oneself).*

Subject pronoun	Reflexive pronoun	Verb
je	me	lave
tu	te	laves
il	se	lave
elle	se	lave
nous	nous	lavons
vous	vous	lavez
ils	se	lavent
elles	se	lavent

The subject pronoun and the reflexive pronoun remain the same, regardless of the tense of the verb: **je me laverai** *(future);* **ils se sont lavés** *(passé composé).*

In addition, you will have to learn the rules of agreement of the past participles of reflexive verbs. They are different from those of other past participles. We refer you to your French grammar book for these rules.

Reflexive verbs are more common in French than in English; that is, there are many verbs that take a reflexive pronoun in French though not in English.

For instance, when you say in English, *"Paul shaved"* it is understood, but not stated, that *"Paul shaved himself."* In French, the *himself* has to be stated. The English verb *to get up* also has a reflexive meaning: *"Mary got up"* means that she got herself up. In French, you have to express *to get up* by using the verb **lever** with its reflexive pronoun **se**. Similarly, some English expressions, such as *to go to bed* are expressed in French by a reflexive verb, in this case **se coucher**. You must memorize these reflexive verbs as they appear.

<< What is Meant by Active Voice and Passive Voice? >>

They are terms used to describe the relationship between the verb and its subject.

The **active voice**: A verb is active when it expresses an action performed by the subject.

> The girl throws the ball.
> S   V   DO

> The child eats the apple.
> S   V   DO

> Lightning strikes the tree.
> S   V   DO

In all these examples, the subject (S) performs the action of the verb (V) and the direct object (DO) is the receiver of the action.

The **passive voice**: A verb is passive when it describes the result of the action occurring in the active sentence.

> The ball is thrown by the girl.
> S   V   Agent

> The apple is eaten by the child.
> S   V   Agent

> The tree is struck by lightning.
> S   V   Agent

In all these examples, the subject is not the performer of the action but is having the action performed upon it. Note also that the tense of the sentence is indicated by the tense of the auxiliary *to be*: "The ball *is* thrown by the girl" is in the present tense; whereas, "The ball *was* thrown by the girl" is in the past tense.

In French: An active sentence can be changed to the passive in exactly the same way as in English.

---

*The girl **throws** the ball.* → *The ball is thrown by the girl.*

La fille **jette** la balle. → La balle **est** jetée par la fille.

    S   V   DO   S   V   Agent
       présent   présent

You should note that:

- All verbs in the passive take the auxiliary **être**. "La fille **a jeté** la balle" is an active sentence with the verb in the **passé composé**; whereas, "la balle **est jetée** par la fille" is a passive sentence with the verb **être** *in the present + the past participle of the main verb.*

- The tense of passive sentences is shown by the tense of the verb **être**.

    La balle **est** jetée.   *The ball is thrown.*
         /
      présent

    La balle **a été** jetée.   *The ball was thrown.*
        /
     passé composé

    La balle **sera** jetée.   *The ball will be thrown.*
        /
     futur

Because the auxiliary is always **être** in the passive, all the past participles agree in gender and number with the subject.

The ball is thrown by the girl.

La balle est jetée par la fille.
  /   /
fém. sing.   fém. sing.

French wines are appreciated the world over.

Les vins français sont appréciés dans le monde entier.
  /   /
masc. pl.   masc. pl.

The French language, however, does not favor the passive voice as English does, and whenever possible French speakers try to avoid the passive by replacing it with an active construction. This is particularly true for general statements:

> English is spoken.
>
> The New York Times is sold here.
>
> In France, stamps are sold in tobacco shops.

We will study how these passive sentences can be transformed into active sentences in French:

- using the "**on**" construction

    The word **on** corresponds to the English indefinite pronoun *one*, such as in the sentence "One should eat when one is hungry."

    To avoid the passive construction, French often makes *one* the subject of an active sentence.

English is spoken in many countries. → One speaks English in many countries.

The New York Times is sold here. → One sells the New York Times here.

In France, stamps are bought in tobacco shops. → In France, one buys stamps in tobacco shops.

Once you have transformed the English passive sentence into the active form with *one*, write it in French.

One speaks English in many countries.
On parle anglais dans beaucoup de pays.

One sells the New York Times here.
On vend le New York Times ici.

In France, one buys stamps in tobacco shops.

En France, on achète les timbres chez un marchand de tabac.

- using the *reflexive construction*

To *reflect* the action back to the subject, the main verb of the sentence is written in its reflexive form (see **What is a Reflexive Verb?** p. 62). This construction can only be used when the doer of the action (the agent) is unimportant.

English is spoken in many countries. → *English speaks *itself* in many countries.

The New York Times is sold here. → *The New York Times sells *itself*.

In France, stamps are bought in tobacco shops. → *In France, stamps buy *themselves* in tobacco shops.

Once you have transformed the English passive sentence into the active form with a reflexive verb, write it in French:

English speaks itself in many countries.

L'anglais se parle dans beaucoup de pays.

The New York Times sells itself here.

Le New York Times se vend ici.

In France, stamps buy themselves in tobacco shops.

En France, les timbres s'achètent chez un marchand de tabac.

---

*An asterisk before a sentence means the sentence is ungrammatical. The purpose of including such a sentence is to compare it to the French one.

<< What is an Adjective? >>

An **adjective** is a word that describes a noun or a pronoun. Be sure that you do not confuse an adjective with a pronoun. A pronoun replaces a noun, while an adjective must always have a noun or a pronoun to describe.

In English: Adjectives describe nouns in many ways. They can tell:

- *what kind* of noun it is — **descriptive adjective**

    She lived in a *large* house.

    He has *lovely brown* eyes.

- *whose* noun it is — **possessive adjective**

    His book is lost.

    Our parents are away.

- *which* noun is it? — **interrogative adjective**

    What book is lost?

    Which newspaper do you want?

- *which* noun it is — **demonstrative adjective**

    This teacher is excellent.

    That question is very appropriate.

In all these cases, it is said that the adjective modifies the noun.

There are also many examples of **nouns used as adjectives**.

Leather is expensive.   *Leather* goods are expensive.
   /   /
  noun   adjective

The *desk* is black.   The *desk* lamp is black.
   /   /
  noun   adjective

In French: Adjectives are identified in the same way as in English. The most important difference is that when an adjective modifies a noun, that adjective must agree with the noun; that is, it must correspond in gender and number with the noun it describes.

Looking only at **descriptive adjectives** for the time being, look at the agreement of the adjective in the following examples:

the blue book   le livre **bleu**
                /   /
      masc. sing.   masc. sing.

the blue dress   la robe **bleue**
              /   /
    fém. sing.   fém. sing.

the blue books   les livres **bleus**
             /   /
    masc. pl.   masc. pl.

the blue dresses   les robes **bleues**
             /   /
    fém. pl.   fém. pl.

NOTE: When a noun is used as an adjective, it remains a noun and does <u>not</u> agree with the noun it describes.

| *the kitchen tables* | les tables de cuisine |
| | fém. pl.   fém. sing. |

| *the chemistry books* | les livres de chimie |
| | masc. pl.   fém. sing. |

| *the French class* | la classe de français |
| | fém. sing.   masc. sing. |

Because of their importance and complexity **possessive adjectives, interrogative adjectives, demonstrative adjectives,** are discussed in separate sections. See pp. 70-79.

<< What is a Possessive Adjective? >>

A **possessive adjective** is a word which describes a noun by showing who possesses it.

In English: Here is a list of the possessive adjectives:

my	our
your	your
his, her, its	their

The possessive adjective refers to the person who possesses.

John's mother is young. *His* mother is young.

Mary's father is rich. *Her* father is rich.

The cat's ears are short. *Its* ears are short.

In French: The possessive adjective refers to and describes the object or person which is possessed (not, as in English, to the person who possesses). Like all adjectives in French, the possessive adjective must agree in number and gender with the <u>noun</u> it modifies, and not with the possessor. The complete list of possessive adjectives is not given here. You will need to consult your French grammar book.

Compare the agreement of possessive adjectives in English and in French:

		Possessive form in French
English:	**Paul** talks to **his** brother.	
French:	Paul talks to ***his brother.***	**son frère**
English:	**Mary** talks to **her** brother.	
French:	Mary talks to **her brother.**	**son frère**
English:	**He** talks to **his** sister.	
French:	He talks to **his sister.**	**sa soeur**
English:	**She** talks to **her** sister.	
French:	She talks to ***her sister.***	**sa soeur**
English:	**He** talks to **his** brothers.	
French:	He talks to ***his brothers.***	**ses frères**
English:	**She** talks to **her** brothers.	
French:	She talks to ***her brothers.***	**ses frères**

A. The possessive adjectives for *my, your* (**tu** form) and *his, her, its* each have a different masculine and feminine form in the singular. Therefore, in the case of *"his brother,"* the *his* will be masculine singular because the word *brother* is masculine singular (**son frère**). In the case of *"his sister,"* the word for *his* will be feminine singular because *sister* is feminine singular (**sa soeur**). In the plural, however, the adjective is the same in the masculine and feminine forms (**ses frères** and **ses soeurs**).

Here are the steps you should follow to choose the correct possessive adjective:

1. Indicate the possessor. In French, this will be shown by the first letter of the possessive adjective.

my	the first letter will be	**m-**
your **tu** *form*	the first letter will be	**t-**
his *her* *its*	the first letter will be	**s-**

I read *my* book.	I read *my* books.
m-	**m-**
You read *your* book.	You read *your* books.
t-	**t-**
She reads *her* book.	She reads *her* books.
s-	**s-**

2. Fill in the possessive adjective so that it will agree in gender and number with the object or person possessed. Start by analyzing the number of the object possessed.

   • If it is plural, just add **-es** to the first letter you found under step 1.

   Livres *is plural.*

Je lis mes livres.	*I read **my** books.*
Tu lis tes livres.	*You read **your** books.*
Elle lit ses livres.	*She read **her** books.*

   • If it is singular, you need to know if the object possessed is masculine or feminine.

Add **-on** — if it is masculine or if it is feminine beginning with a vowel.

Livre *is masculine singular.*

Je lis **mon** livre.	*I read **my** book.*
Tu lis **ton** livre.	*You read **your** book.*
Elle lit **son** livre.	*She reads **her** book.*

Amie *is feminine but begins with a vowel.*

Paul rencontre **son** amie. *Paul meets **his** friend.*

Add **-a** — if it is feminine.

Lettre *is feminine singular.*

Je lis **ma** lettre.	*I read **my** letter.*
Tu lis **ta** lettre.	*You read **your** letter.*
Elle lit **sa** lettre.	*She reads **her** letter.*

B. The possessive adjectives for *our, your* (**vous** *form*) and *their* are much easier to use because it's necessary only to identify the object or person possessed as being singular or plural.

- If it is singular, choose between **notre, votre, leur.**

Paul est **notre** garçon.	*Paul is **our** boy.*
Hélène est **notre** fille.	*Helen is **our** girl.*
Vous lisez **votre** livre.	*You read **your** book.*
Vous lisez **votre** lettre.	*You read **your** letter.*
Ils lisent **leur** livre.	*They read **their** book.*
Elles lisent **leur** lettre.	*They read **their** letter.*

- If it is plural, choose between **nos, vos, leurs.**

Paul et Hélène sont **nos** enfants.   *Paul and Helen are **our** children.*

Vous lisez **vos** livres.   *You read **your** books.*

Elles lisent **leurs** lettres.   *They read **their** letters.*

In French and in English, the subject and the possessive adjective do not necessarily match. It all depends on what you want to say.

Avez-**vous** mon livre?   *Do **you** have **my** book?*
/   /   /   /
2nd person   *1st person*   *2nd person*   *1st person*

Avez-**vous** apporté **leurs** cadeaux?   *Did **you** bring **their** gifts?*
/   /   /   /
2nd person   *3rd person*   *2nd person*   *3rd person*

NOTE: Before you write a sentence with *your*, decide if it is appropriate to use the **tu** *form* or the **vous** *form* in French. Then, make sure that your sentence is entirely in that form; for example, if your verb is in the **tu** *form*, the possessive adjective must be in the **tu** *form:* "**Tu** lis **ta** lettre." On the other hand, if your verb is in the **vous** *form,* the possessive adjective must be in the **vous** *form:* "**Vous** lisez **votre** lettre." Be consistent as you cannot mix the two forms.

NOTES:

<< What is an Interrogative Adjective? >>

An **interrogative adjective** is a word which asks a question about a noun.

In English: The words *which* and *what* are called interrogative adjectives when they come in front of a noun and are used to ask a question.

> *Which* book do you want?

> *What* dress do you want to wear?

In French: The interrogative adjective is **quel**, which changes to agree with the noun it modifies. Therefore, in order to say *"which book"* or *"what dress"* in French, you start by determining the gender and number of the word *book* or *dress*.

- *What book is on the table?*

> **Livre** is *masculine singular,* so that the word for "what" is also masculine singular.

Quel livre est sur la table?
masc. sing.   masc. sing.

- *What books are on the table?*

> **Livres** is *masculine plural,* so that the word for "what" is also masculine plural.

Quels livres sont sur la table?
masc. pl.   masc. pl.

- *What dress are you wearing?*

> **Robe** is *feminine singular,* so that the word for "what" is feminine singular.

Quelle robe portez-vous?
fém. sing. fém. sing.

- *What dresses do you want?*

> **Robes** is *feminine plural,* so that the word for "what" is feminine plural.

Quelles robes voulez-vous?
fém. pl. fém. pl.

The interrogative adjective is also used to express the English *what* or *which* in sentences such as these:

- *What is your favorite sport?*

Quel est votre **sport** préféré?
masc. sing. masc. sing.

- *What are his favorite programs?*

Quels sont ses **programmes** préférés?
masc. pl. masc. pl.

- *Which is their classroom?*

Quelle est leur **salle** de classe?
fém. sing. fém. sing.

If you are not certain whether *what* or *which* is an interrogative adjective in sentences such as the ones above, try putting the word *what* or *which* in front of the noun and change the sentence to read as follows:

> *What* is your favorite sport? → *What sport* is your favorite?

You can see that the second sentence is only a variation of the first. The meaning and the function of the words are identical. Therefore in French, the word **quel** that occurs before the masculine singular word **sport** "quel sport," is the same **quel** that occurs in the sentence "**Quel est votre sport préféré?**" Here are more examples:

• *What is your address?*

> *What* is your address? → *What address* is yours?

Quelle est votre **adresse?**
   /   /
fém. sing.   fém. sing.

• *What are your favorite books?*

> *What* are your favorite books? → *What books* are your favorite?

Quels sont vos **livres** préférés?
   /   /
masc. pl.   masc. pl.

NOTE: The word *what* in "*What* is on the table?" is an interrogative pronoun. It has a different function, and hence a different form in French, from the interrogative adjective *what* that occurs in "*What* book is on the table?" (See **What are Interrogative Pronouns?** p. 103.)

<< What is a Demonstrative Adjective? >>

A **demonstrative adjective** is a word used to *point out* a noun.

In English: The demonstrative adjectives are ***this, that, these*** and ***those***. They are a rare example of adjectives agreeing with the noun they modify: ***this*** changes to ***these*** before a plural noun and ***that*** changes to ***those***.

> ***this*** cat   ***these*** cats

> ***that*** man   ***those*** men

In French: Demonstrative adjectives have a singular and a plural form. In the singular, they are either masculine or feminine, depending on the gender of the noun they modify. In the plural, the same form is used for both masculine and feminine nouns.

If you want to say "***this*** or ***that*** room" in French, you start by analyzing the word *room.*

> ***this (or that) room***

> > **Chambre** is *feminine singular*, so that the word for *this/ that* is also feminine singular.

> **cette** chambre
>   /   /
> fém. sing.   fém. sing.

Similarly for "***this*** or ***that*** book" start by analyzing the word *book.*

> ***this (or that) book***

> > **Livre** is *masculine singular*, so that the word for *this/that* is also masculine singular.

> **ce** livre
> /   /
> masc. sing. masc. sing.

Since the plural form for both genders is **ces**, it is sufficient to identify "*these* (or *those*) books" and "*these* (or *those*) rooms" as plurals.

ces livres   **ces** chambres
  /   /   /   /
 pl. masc. pl.   pl.   fém. pl.

<< What is an Adverb? >>

An **adverb** is a word that modifies (describes) a verb, an adjective or another adverb. Adverbs indicate quantity, time, place, intensity and manner.

Mary drives *well*.
       /
     verb

The house is *very* big.
              /
          adjective

The girl ran *too* quickly.
              /
          adverb

In English: Here are some examples of adverbs:

- of quantity or degree

  Mary sleeps *little*.
  Bob does well *enough* in class.

  These adverbs answer the question *how much*.

- of time

  He will come *soon*.
  The children are *late*.

  These adverbs answer the question *when*.

- of place

> The teacher looked *around.*
> The old were left *behind.*

These adverbs answer the question *where.*

- of intensity

> Bob *really* wants to learn French.
> Mary can *actually* read Latin.

These adverbs are used for *emphasis.*

- of manner

> Bob sings *beautifully.*
> They parked the car *carefully.*

These adverbs answer the question *how.* They are the most common adverbs and can usually be recognized by their *-ly* ending.

In French: You will have to memorize most adverbs as vocabulary items. Most adverbs of manner can be recognized by the ending **-ment.**

joli**ment**	*beautifully*
complète**ment**	*completely*
heureuse**ment**	*happily*

The most important thing for you to remember is that adverbs are **invariable**: this means that the spelling never changes. (Adverbs never become plural, nor do they have a gender.) For this reason, it is necessary that you distinguish adverbs from adjectives which do change. When you write a sentence in French, always make sure that the adjectives agree with the noun or pronoun they modify, and that adverbs remain unchanged.

- *The **tall** girl sang **beautifully***.

    Tall modifies the noun *girl*; it is an adjective.

    Beautifully modifies the verb *sang*; it describes how she sang; it is an adverb.

La **grande fille** chantait **joliment**.
/   /   /
fém. sing.   fém. sing.   *adverb*

- *The **tall** boy sang **beautifully***.

    Tall modifies the noun *boy*; it is an adjective.

    Beautifully modifies the verb *sang*; it describes how he sang; it is an adverb.

Le **grand garçon** chantait **joliment**.
/   /   /
masc. sing.   masc. sing.   *adverb*

<<   What is a Preposition?   >>

A **preposition** is a word which shows the relationship between a noun and another word in the sentence. Prepositions indicate position, direction or time.

In English: Here are examples of some prepositions:

- to show position
    Bob was *in* the car.
    The books are *on* the table.

- to show direction
    Mary went *to* school.
    The students came directly *from* class.

- to show time
    French people go on vacation *in* August.
    Their son will be home *at* Christmas.

82

In French: You will have to memorize prepositions as vocabulary items. There are three important things to remember:

1. Prepositions are **invariable**. This means that their spelling never changes. (They never become plural, nor do they have a gender.)

2. Prepositions are tricky little words. Every language uses prepositions differently. Do not assume that the same preposition is used in French as in English, or that one is even used at all.

English	*French*
preposition → no preposition	
to look *for*	chercher
to look *at*	regarder
no preposition → preposition	
to telephone	téléphoner *à*
to ask	demander *à*
change of preposition	
to be angry *with*	être fâché *contre* (against)
to be *on* the plane	être *dans* l'avion (in)

3. Although the position of a preposition in an English sentence may vary, it cannot in French. Look at the position of the preposition in the following English sentences:

Spoken English	*Formal English*
The man I speak *to*.	→ The man *to* whom I speak.
Who are you playing *with*?	→ *With* whom are you playing?
The teacher I'm talking *about*.	→ The teacher *about* whom I'm talking.

Spoken English tends to place the preposition at the end of the sentence. Formal English places the preposition within the sentence or at the beginning of a question.

The position of a preposition in a French sentence is the same as in formal English; that is, it is <u>never</u> at the end of a sentence. Whenever you have a preposition at the end of an English sentence, be sure to change the structure.

There are some English expressions where the natural position of the preposition is at the end of the sentence; it is not a question of spoken or written language.

We have much to be thankful *for.*

Changing the structure of the above sentence to place the preposition within the sentence gives an awkward sentence.

We have much *for* which to be thankful.

However, in French, it is still necessary to reword the sentence to include the preposition within the sentence. This rearranging of the preposition will be very helpful to you. It will help you to determine the function of words and the word order in the French sentence.

NOTE: A special word needs to be said about the preposition **de** *(of, from, etc.)* in French, because it is used in structures that do not exist in English.

1. When a noun is used as an adjective to describe another noun (see p. 69), **de** is used as follows:

- the noun described + **de** + the noun which describes *without* an article

A	B
les tables **de** cuisine	*the kitchen tables*
les livres **de** chimie	*the chemistry books*
la classe **de** français	*the French class*

The noun in Column B gives information about the noun in Column A.

2. When a noun possesses another noun (see p. 14), **de** is used as follows:

- the noun possessed + **de** + definite article + the noun that possesses

A	B	
le sac **de la** dame	*the lady's handbag*	
la couleur **de la** robe	*the dress's color*	
les branches **de l'**arbre	*the tree's branches*	
la bicyclette **du** garçon	*the boy's bicycle*	

/
de + le → du

la longueur **du** livre	*the book's length*
le club **des** filles	*the girls' club*

/
de + les → des

le professeur **des** étudiants   *the students' teacher*

The noun in Column A belongs to the noun in Column B.

3. When indicating a quantity of a noun, **de** is used as follows:

- the quantity + **de** + the noun *without* an article

A	B
une douzaine **d'**oeufs	*a dozen eggs*
beaucoup **d'**étudiants	*many students*
une livre **de** beurre	*a pound of butter*

The noun in Column A indicates a quantity of the noun in Column B.

<< What is a Conjunction? >>

A **conjunction** is a word which joins words or groups of words.

> Paul plays basketball *and* tennis.
> We'll go to the movies *or* the theater.
> I liked neither the book *nor* the play.
> The children are happy *whenever* he comes.

Conjunctions are to be memorized as vocabulary items. Remember that like adverbs and prepositions, conjunctions are **invariable**; they never change. (They never become plural, nor do they have a gender.)

NOTES:

< < What are Objects? > >

Every sentence consists, at the very least, of a subject and a verb. This is called the **sentence base**.

> Children play.
>
> Work stopped.

Many verbs, however, call for another word to indicate the person or thing that the action of the subject is directed toward. This receiver of the action is called an **object**. These objects are divided into three categories according to the word which separates the verb from the receiver. The three kinds of objects are:

1. direct object
2. indirect object
3. object of a preposition

1. **Direct Object:** It receives the action of the verb or shows the result of that action directly, without prepositions separating the verb from the receiver. It answers the *one-word question "what?"* or *"whom?"* asked *after* the verb.

> Paul takes *the book.*
>
> > Paul takes *what*? The book.
> >
> > *The book* is the direct object.

> They meet *Paul and Mary.*
>
> > They meet *whom*? Paul and Mary.
> >
> > *Paul and Mary* are the two direct objects.

Never assume that a word is the direct object. Always ask the one-word question and if you don't get an answer, you don't have a direct object in the sentence.

2. **Indirect Objects:** It also receives the action of the verb or shows the result of that action. However, it receives the action indirectly; that is, the verb needs the preposition " *to* " ("à") to indicate the receiver of the action or the result of the action. It answers the *two-word question* *"to whom"* or *"to what"* asked *after* the verb.

> Paul speaks *to the teacher.*

>> Paul speaks *to whom?* To the teacher.
>> *To the teacher* is the indirect object.

> Mary writes to *her brother and sister.*

>> Mary writes *to whom?* To her brother and to her
>>> sister.
>> *To her brother* and *to her sister* are the two indirect objects.

In French: Now that we have looked at direct and indirect objects in English, let's observe them in French. Since indirect objects in French are <u>always</u> preceded by the preposition "à", they are easier to identify than in English. As a result, those objects that are not preceded by a preposition are direct objects.

- Direct objects:

> *Paul takes **the book.***
> Paul prend **le livre.**

> *They meet **Paul and Mary.***
> Ils rencontrent **Paul et Marie.**

- Indirect objects:

> *Paul speaks **to the teacher.***
> Paul parle **au professeur.**
>
> $$\boxed{\text{à + le} \rightarrow \text{au}}$$

> *Mary writes **to her brother and sister.***
> Marie écrit **à son frère** et **à sa soeur.**

Some verbs can take both a direct and an indirect object.

In English: There are two patterns for sentences containing a direct and an indirect object:

1. subject + verb + direct object +" *to* "+ indirect object
   Mark   sends   flowers   to   Caroline.

       Mark sends *what?* Flowers.
       Flowers is the *direct object.*

       Mark sends flowers *to whom?* To Caroline.
       To Caroline is the *indirect object.*

2. subject + verb + indirect object + direct object
   Mark   sends   Caroline   flowers.

       Mark sends *what?* Flowers.
       Flowers is the *direct object.*

       Mark sends flowers *to whom?* To Caroline.
       To Caroline is the *indirect object.*

As you can see, the position of the direct and indirect objects has changed in sentence 2. *"Caroline"* is still the indirect object (because it still answers the question *"to whom?"*), but now it occurs before the direct object, *"flowers,"* without the preposition *to.*

In French: There is only one pattern for sentences containing a direct and an indirect object, as long as both the objects are nouns. (In the case when the objects are pronouns, the pattern in French is different. See **What is a Personal Object Pronoun?**, p. 92.) The pattern is the same as number 1 above.

    subject + verb + direct object + "à" *+ indirect object*
    Marc   envoie   des fleurs   à   Caroline.

Make sure that you place the direct object before the indirect object.

3. **Object of a Preposition:** It also receives the action of the verb or shows the result of that action. Only it receives it indirectly; that is, the verb needs a preposition (other than *"to"* which introduces an indirect object), such as *with, without, behind,* etc. It answers a *two-word question* made up of the *"preposition + what or whom"*; for instance, *with whom, with what, without whom, without what,* etc. asked *after* the verb.

> He comes with *Paul.*

>> He comes *with whom?* With Paul.
>> *Paul* is the object of the preposition *with.*

> John is behind *the tree.*

>> John is *behind what?* Behind the tree.
>> *The tree* is the object of the preposition *behind.*

In French: Objects of a preposition are as easy to identify as in English. The above two sentences in French read as follows:

>> *He comes with Paul.*
>> Il vient **avec Paul.**

>> *John is behind the tree.*
>> Jean est **derrière l'arbre.**

Make sure that you recognize prepositions in French.

Objects in summary:

The different types of objects in a sentence are identified according to whether or not they are introduced by a preposition and, if so, which one.

If the action of the verb goes directly to the object without a preposition, the object is called **direct.**

If the action of the verb goes to the object through the preposition *to*, the object is called **indirect.**

If the action of the verb goes to the object through a preposition other than *to*, the object is called **object of a preposition.**

In French: Your ability to recognize the three kinds of objects is essential when using pronouns. Three different pronouns are used for the single English word *them*, for example, depending upon whether *them* is a direct object (**les**), an indirect object (**leur**), or the object of a preposition (**eux**).

As a student of French, you must watch out for the following pitfall: some English verbs that take a direct object in English may take an indirect object in French, and some English verbs that take an indirect object in English take a direct object in French. This happens because a verb may need a preposition in one language and not in the other. You should be on the lookout for these verbs and remember what distinguishes them from English:

- *to obey* – **obéir à**

  *Paul obeys his **mother**.*

  > Paul obeys whom? His mother.
  > ***Mother*** is the *direct object.*

  Paul obéit **à sa mère.**

  > Paul obéit à qui? A sa mère.
  > **A sa mère** is the *indirect object.*

- *to wait for* – **attendre**

  *Paul waits **for his mother**.*

  > Paul waits *for* whom? For his mother.
  > ***Mother*** is the *object of the preposition for.*

  Paul attend **sa mère.**

  > Paul attend qui? Sa mère.
  > **Mère** is the *direct object.*

- *to listen to* — **écouter**

   Paul listens *to his mother.*

   Paul listens *to* whom? To his mother.
   Mother is the *indirect object.*

   Paul écoute **sa mère.**

   Paul écoute qui? Sa mère.
   Mère is the *direct object.*

Here are some other verbs to watch out for:

   *to look **for*** — chercher
   *to look **at*** — regarder
   to obey (someone) — obéir **à**
   to answer — répondre **à**
   to telephone — téléphoner **à**

   ———————

NOTES:

<< What is a Personal Object Pronoun? >>

Personal pronouns, in English and in French, change according to their function in the sentence. Personal pronouns used as *subject* of a sentence are studied on p. 23.

Let's look at pronouns used as *objects*.

In English: The pronouns that occur as objects in a sentence are different from the ones used as subjects. The former are called **object pronouns**. They are used when the pronoun is either the *direct* or *indirect object*, as well as *the object of a preposition* (see p. 86).

> *He and I* work for the newspaper.
> /
> subject — subject pronouns

> Mother called *me and him* for dinner.
> /
> direct object — object pronouns

> I lent my car *to them.*
> /
> indirect object — object pronoun

> They are coming with *you and me.*
> /
> object of a preposition — object pronouns

Compare the English pronouns:

Subject	*Object*
I	me
you	you
he	him
she	her
it	it
we	us
you	you
they	them

In French: Let's refresh your memory with the **personal pronouns used as the subject** of the sentence (the equivalent of the English subject pronouns).

je	*1st pers. sing.*
tu	*2nd pers. sing.*
il	*3rd pers. sing.*
elle	
nous	*1st pers. pl.*
vous	*2nd pers. pl.*
ils	*3rd pers. pl.*
elles	

Remember that the French equivalent for *it* is either **il** or **elle** depending upon whether *it* replaces a masculine or feminine noun.

In French, the same **personal pronoun** is used both **as a direct and an indirect object**, except for the 3rd person singular **(il, elle)** and the 3rd person plural **(ils, elles)**. Let's look at the 1st and 2nd persons:

Subject	*Object*
je	me
tu	te
—	—
nous	nous
vous	vous
—	—

The fact that **nous** and **vous** can stand for both subject and object of a sentence is sometimes confusing. The reason is that both direct and indirect object pronouns, just like subjects, occur <u>before</u> the verb in French, not after it. Don't think of these pronouns only as subjects. In case of doubt, look at the verb; remember that verbs agree with their subject. If **nous** is the subject, the verb will end in "**-ons;**" if it doesn't, **nous** is an object of some kind. The same is true with **vous**. If it is the subject of the verb, the ending of regular verbs will be "**-ez.**"

- Le vendeur **nous** regarde.
  (The salesman is looking at us.)

> **Nous** cannot be the subject. The subject of "regarde" must be a 3rd person singular, in this case **le vendeur. Nous** is a direct object.

- Les vendeurs **vous** montrent la marchandise.
  (The salesmen are showing you the merchandise.)

> **Vous** cannot be the subject of "montrent." The subject of "montrent" must be a 3rd person plural, in this case **les vendeurs. Vous** is an indirect object. (**La marchandise** is the direct object.)

The personal pronouns of the 3rd person, the ones that are the equivalent of *him, her, it, them,* change according to whether they are used as direct or indirect objects and according to the gender and number of the noun they replace.

		Subject	Direct Object	Indirect Object
singular	*masculine*	il	le	lui
	feminine	elle	la	lui
plural	*masculine*	ils	les	leur
	feminine	elles	les	leur

It in French can be (1) a subject or direct object, (2) masculine or feminine. You must, therefore, establish its function and the gender of the noun it replaces.

- *Where is the book?* ***It*** *is on the table.*

> Function: subject of *is*
> Noun it replaces: the book
> Gender in French: masculine **(le livre)**

Therefore *it* = **il**.

Où est le livre? **Il** est sur la table.

- *Where is the table?* ***It*** *is in the room.*

> Function: subject of *is*
> Noun it replaces: the table
> Gender in French: feminine **(la table)**

Therefore *it* = **elle**.

Où est la table? **Elle** est dans la chambre.

- *Do you see the book? Yes, I see* ***it.***

> Function: direct object
> Noun it replaces: the book
> Gender in French: masculine **(le livre)**

Therefore *it* = **le**.

Voyez-vous le livre? Oui, je **le** vois.

- *Do you see the table? Yes, I see* ***it.***

> Function: direct object
> Noun it replaces: the table
> Gender in French: feminine **(la table)**

Therefore *it* = **la**.

Voyez-vous la table? Oui, je **la** vois.

Him or *her* can be (1) a direct object or (2) an indirect object. You must determine if it is a direct or indirect object *in French*. See pp. 87 & 90-91.

- *Do you see Paul? Yes, I see **him**.*
  *Do you see Mary? Yes, I see **her**.*

> Function: direct object
> Therefore *him* = **le**
> and   *her* = **la**.

Voyez-vous Paul? Oui, je **le** vois.
Voyez-vous Marie? Oui, je **la** vois.

- *Are you giving Paul the book? Yes, I am giving **him** the book.*
  *Are you giving Mary the book? Yes, I am giving **her** the book.*

> Function: indirect object (I give the book *to whom? To* him, *to* her.) *The book* is the direct object.
> Therefore *him* = **lui**
> and   *her* = **lui**.

Donnez-vous le livre à Paul? Oui, je **lui** donne le livre.
Donnez-vous le livre à Marie? Oui, je **lui** donne le livre.

The only way you can tell if **lui** refers to a girl or a boy is from what has been said before.

Them can be (1) a direct object, or (2) an indirect object. You must establish if it is a direct or indirect object *in French*.

- *Do you see Paul and Mary? Yes, I see **them**.*

> Function: direct object
> Therefore *them* = **les**.

Voyez-vous Paul et Marie? Oui, je **les** vois.

- *Do you give Paul and Mary the book?*

  *Yes, I give **them** the book.*

> Function: indirect object (I give the book *to whom? To them.*) *The book* is the direct object.
> Therefore ***them*** = **leur**.

Donnez-vous le livre à Paul et à Marie?

Oui, je **leur** donne le livre.

NOTE: When the pronoun *it* or ***them*** is an indirect object and replaces a noun which does <u>not</u> refer to a person, the pronoun y is used for both the singular and the plural.

- Je réponds **à sa lettre.**   *I answer his/her letter.*

  | à + *thing sing.* → y |

  J'y réponds.   *I answer **it**.*

but Je réponds **à sa mère.**   *I answer his/her mother.*

  | à + *person sing.* → lui |

  Je **lui** réponds.   *I answer **him/her**.*

- J'obéis **aux lois.**   *I obey the laws.*

  | à + *thing pl.* → y |

  J'y obéis.   *I obey **them**.*

but J'obéis **à mes parents.**   *I obey my parents.*

  | à + *person pl.* → leur |

  Je **leur** obéis.   *I obey **them**.*

NOTE: You must make this distinction when you replace indirect objects in the third person.

98

Once again we remind you that the direct object and an indirect object must be determined in the French sentence.

Direct object in English — Indirect object in French

- *Does Mary obey **her parents**?*

  *Yes, she obeys **them**.*

  direct object *(Mary obeys whom? Her parents.)*

  Function in English: direct object

  However, the French verb is **obéir** à. Therefore, there is a preposition between the verb and the object making the object indirect.

  Est-ce que Marie obéit **à ses parents?**

  Oui, elle **leur** obéit.

  indirect object (Marie obéit à qui? A ses parents.)

  Function in French: indirect object

- *Does Paul telephone **his friend**?*

  *Yes, he telephones **him**.*

  direct object *(Paul telephones whom? His friend.)*

  Function in English: direct object

  However, the French verb is **téléphoner** à. Therefore, there is a preposition between the verb and the object making the object indirect.

  Est-ce que Paul téléphone **à son ami?**

  Oui, il **lui** téléphone.

  indirect object (Paul téléphone à qui? A son ami.)

  Function in French: indirect object

For a list of additional verbs that take different types of object in English and in French see pp. 90-91.

Personal pronouns in summary:

Make sure that you can recognize a personal pronoun and then follow these steps:

   1. Determine the function of the pronoun in French:

   • Is it the subject?
   • Is it the direct object?
   • Is it the indirect object?

   In the case of the 3rd person also ask:

   • Does it replace a person or thing?
   • If it is a singular person, is it masculine or feminine?

   2. If there are two pronouns, one a direct object and one an indirect object:

   • Proceed as outlined under 1. above for each pronoun individually.

   • Place them in correct order before the verb. (Consult your French grammar book for the order of pronouns.)

We have now looked at personal pronouns that are subjects of a sentence, direct objects of a sentence and indirect objects of a sentence. In all these cases, the pronoun either directly follows the verb in English or is separated from it by the preposition *to*, in the case of *to + indirect object*. **Personal pronouns which stand alone** or which are separated from the verb by a preposition other than the indirect object *to* are called **disjunctive, emphatic** or **stressed pronouns**.

Who is there? *Me.*
/
Personal pronoun used alone.

I am going with *him.*
/
Personal pronoun object of the preposition *with.*

In English: The same personal objects are used for direct objects, indirect objects and objects of a preposition.

In French: A different set of personal pronouns is used for direct and indirect objects (see p. 93 & 94), as well as for objects of a preposition. The same pronouns that occur as objects of a preposition are also used when the pronoun stands alone. They are called **pronoms personnels toniques.**

Let's look at these three sets side by side so you can see where they differ:

	Direct Object	Indirect Object	Disjunctive Pronouns
1st per. sing.	me	me	moi
2nd per. sing.	te	te	toi
3rd per. sing. masc.	le	lui	lui
fem.	la	lui	elle
1st per. pl.	nous	nous	nous
2nd per. pl.	vous	vous	vous
3rd per. pl. masc.	les	leur	eux
fem.	les	leur	elles

You will use a disjunctive pronoun in the following cases:

1. When a personal pronoun is used alone, usually to answer a question.

   Qui est là? **Moi.**   *Who is there? **Me.***

   Qui a pris le livre? **Lui.**   *Who took the book? **Him.***

2. When a personal pronoun is used after a preposition other than the indirect *to.*

   *Is the book for Paul? No it's for **me.***

   __Me__ is object of the preposition for.

   Est-ce que le livre est pour Paul? Non, il est pour **moi.**

There is an additional step when you use a disjunctive pronoun of the 3rd person singular or the 3rd person plural: You must determine the *gender* and the *number* of the noun it replaces.

- *Are you going to the party with Mary?*
  *Yes, I'm going with **her**.*

  > **Her** is object of the preposition *with*.
  > Noun it replaces: *Mary*
  > Gender and number: *Mary* is feminine singular.

  Est-ce que vous allez à la soirée avec Marie?
  Oui, je vais avec **elle**.
  /
  fém. sing.

- *Are you going to the party with Paul?*
  *Yes, I'm going with **him**.*

  > **Him** is object of the preposition *with*.
  > Noun it replaces: *Paul*
  > Gender and number: *Paul* is masculine singular.

  Est-ce que vous allez à la soirée avec Paul?
  Oui, je vais avec **lui**.
  /
  masc. sing.

- *Are you going to the party with Paul and Henry?*
  *No, I'm going without **them**.*

  > **Them** is object of the preposition *without*.
  > Nouns it replaces: *Paul* and *Henry*
  > Gender and number: *Paul* and *Henry* are masculine plural.

  Est-ce que vous allez à la soirée avec Paul et Henri?
  Non, je vais sans **eux**.
  /
  masc. pl.

102

- *Are you going to the party with Mary and Helen?*
*No, I'm going without **them**.*

> ***Them*** is object of the preposition *without*.
> Nouns it replaces: *Mary* and *Helen*
> Gender and number: *Mary* and *Helen* are
> feminine plural.

Est-ce que vous allez à la soirée avec Marie et Hélène?
Non, je vais sans **elles**.
/
fém. pl.

Once again we remind you that the types of objects must be identified in the French sentence.

Object of a preposition in English – Direct object in French

- *Are you looking **at Paul**?*
*Yes, I'm looking **at him**.*
/
object of a preposition (You are looking at whom? At Paul.)

> Function in English: object of a preposition

> However, the French verb **regarder** means *to look at*. It is therefore <u>not</u> followed by a preposition. Since there is no preposition, the object is direct.

Est-ce que vous regardez Paul?
Oui, je **le** regarde.
/
direct object (Vous regardez qui? Paul.)

> Function in French: direct object

- *Are you looking for Mary?*

  Yes, I'm looking for her.
  /
  object of a preposition *(You are looking for whom?*
  For Mary.)

Function in English: object of a preposition

However, the French verb **chercher** means *to look for*. It is therefore <u>not</u> followed by a preposition. Since there is no preposition, the object is direct.

Est-ce que vous cherchez Marie?

Oui, je **la** cherche.
/
direct object (Vous cherchez qui? Marie.)

Function in French: direct object

<< What is an Interrogative Pronoun? >>

A **pronoun** is a word that stands for one or more nouns. It is a word used instead of a noun. At this point we are going to look at pronouns used to introduce a question; that is, **interrogative pronouns.**

In English: An interrogative pronoun is different if it refers to a person or a thing.

> *What* is on the table?[1]   *refers to a thing*
>
> *Who* is in the room?   *refers to a person*

Whom is used when the interrogative pronoun is the object.

Whom are you waiting for?

Otherwise, *who* and *what* do not change.

---

[1] Do not confuse with "**What** book is on the table?" where *what* is an interrogative adjective. See p. 75.

In French: You must learn to recognize an interrogative pronoun and distinguish it from an interrogative adjective (see p. 75). Once you have identified a word as an interrogative pronoun, proceed with the following two steps in order to find the correct French equivalent.

1. What is the function of the interrogative pronoun in the sentence?

- Is it the subject?
- Is it the direct object?
- Is it the indirect object?
- Is it the object of a preposition?

In the last two cases; i.e., when the pronoun is an indirect object or an object of a preposition, it will be easier for you to determine the function of the pronoun if you go through an extra step. Because in spoken English we usually separate the preposition and the pronoun, you should change this structure to a more formal English structure. Changing the structure will help you to determine the function of the pronoun and to establish the French word order. Look at the following sentences.

Who are you giving the book *to?*
/ /
pronoun   preposition

What are you contributing *to?*
/ /
pronoun   preposition

Who are you going out *with?*
/ /
pronoun   preposition

What are you writing *with?*
/ /
pronoun   preposition

You can see that in each of the above sentences, the preposition is at the end of the sentence, so that it is hard to tell that in each case the pronoun is an *object of a preposition* or an *indirect object pronoun.* If you change the structure by placing the preposition just before the pronoun, it will be much simpler to see the function of the pronoun and to express yourself in French:

Spoken English	Formal English
Who are you giving the book *to?* →	*To whom* are you giving the book?
What are you contributing *to?* →	*To what* are you contributing?
Who are you going out *with?* →	*With whom* are you going out?
What are you writing *with?* →	*With what* are you writing?

In the examples of indirect objects and objects of a preposition below, you will see how much easier it is to work from the more formal English structure in order to write French.

2. Does the pronoun refer to a person or a thing?

In each of the cases listed above a different French pronoun is used. Let's look at an example of each possibility.

• Subject   *who*

   Who speaks French?

    1. Function: *Who* is the subject of the verb *speaks.*

    2. *Who* refers to a person.

In French: **Qui est-ce qui** or **Qui**

Qui parle français?

Qui est-ce qui parle français?

- Subject   *what*

  What is on the table?

  1. Function: *What* is the subject of the verb
     is.
  2. *What* refers to a thing.

  In French: **Qu'est-ce qui**

  Qu'est-ce qui est sur la table?

- Direct object   *who(m)*

  Who(m) do you see?[1]

  1. Function: **Whom** is the direct object of the
     verb *see.*
  2. *Whom* refers to a person.

  In French: **Qui est-ce que** or **Qui** + inversion

  Qui est-ce que vous voyez?
  Qui voyez-vous?
       /
    inversion

  NOTE: In French you can immediately rule out
  the interrogative pronoun as being the subject of
  this sentence. Since the verb is *voyez*, the subject
  must be **vous**. Just as the subject gives you the verb
  form, the verb form tells you what the subject is.
  Learn to associate the two.

---

[1]Who is usually used instead of **whom** in spoken English and in informal written English.

- Direct object   *what*

  What do you see?

  1. Function: *What* is the direct object of the verb *see*.
  2. *What* refers to a thing.

  In French: **Qu'est-ce que** or **Que** + inversion

  Qu'est-ce que vous voyez?
  Que voyez-vous?
  /
  inversion

The next two functions (*indirect object* and *object of a preposition*) involve prepositions. Make sure that you change spoken English to formal English. This will help you to determine function and to establish French word order. (See pp. 82-83.)

- Indirect object   *who(m)*

  Who are you giving the book to?

Who are you giving the book *to*? → *To whom* are you giving the book?

  1. Function: *To whom* is the indirect object of the verb *give*. (*Book* is the direct object.)
  2. *To whom* refers to a person.

  In French: **A qui est-ce que** or **A qui** + inversion

  A qui est-ce que vous donnez le livre?
  A qui donnez-vous le livre?
  /
  inversion

- Indirect object   *what*

  What are you contributing to?

What are you contributing *to?* → *To what* are you contributing?

---

1. Function: *To what* is the indirect object of the verb *contributing.*
2. *To what* refers to something other than a human being.

In French: **A quoi est-ce que** or **A quoi** + inversion

A quoi est-ce que vous contribuez?
A quoi contribuez-vous?
/
inversion

- Object of a preposition   *who(m)*

  Who are you going out with?

Who are you going out *with?* → *With whom* are you going out?

---

1. Function: *Whom* is the object of the preposition *with.*
2. *Whom* refers to a person.

In French: Preposition **(avec) + qui est-ce que** or
Preposition **(avec) + qui** + inversion

Avec qui est-ce que vous sortez ce soir?
Avec qui sortez-vous ce soir?
/
inversion

- Object of a preposition   *what*

  What are you writing with?

| *What* are you writing *with*? → *With what* are you writing? |

---

      1. Function: *What* is the object of the preposition
                with.
      2. *What* refers to a thing.

     In French: Preposition **(avec) + quoi est-ce que** or
                 Preposition **(avec) + quoi** + inversion

Avec quoi est-ce que vous écrivez?

Avec quoi écrivez-vous?
            /
       inversion

Once again, we remind you that some French verbs take direct objects, while the equivalent English verbs take an indirect object and vice-versa. (See pp. 90-91.) Make sure that you determine the function of the pronoun in French, particularly with regard to direct objects, indirect objects and objects of a preposition.

There is another interrogative pronoun which is being studied separately because it does not follow the same pattern.

In English: The interrogative pronoun *which (one, ones)* is used in a question when asking that one (singular) or several (plural) be selected from a group. *One* or *ones* is often omitted.

     Here are two newspapers.
     Which (one) do you want?

     Which (ones) of your friends live in France?

In French: These interrogative pronouns agree in gender with the noun they replace. Their number depends on whether you want to say *which one* (singular) or *which ones* (plural). They are selected from the following series:

lequel	*masc. sing.*	laquelle	*fem. sing.*
lesquels	*masc. pl.*	lesquelles	*fem. pl.*

To select the proper form, follow these steps:

- *Here are three newspapers. **Which one** do you want?*

   1. What noun is ***which*** referring to?
   Newspapers.
   2. What is the gender of *newspapers* in French?
   Journaux is masculine.
   3. Select the form that corresponds to the gender.
   Lequel.
   4. Make the pronoun singular or plural depending on whether you want to say *which one* (singular) or *which ones* (plural).

   In this case it remains singular.

Voici trois journaux. **Lequel** voulez-vous?

- *Which (ones) of these dresses do you want?*

   1. What noun is ***which*** referring to?
   Dresses.
   2. What is the gender of *dresses* in French?
   Robes is feminine.
   3. Select the form that corresponds to the gender.
   Laquelle.
   4. Make the pronoun singular or plural depending on whether you want to say *which one* (singular) or *which ones* (plural).

   In this case it becomes plural.

Lesquelles de ces robes voulez-vous?

Whenever **lequel, lesquels,** or **lesquelles** follow the preposition **à** or **de,** the **le-** and **les-** combine with the preposition. In order to find out if there is a preposition, you must work in French. In some cases, the English expression does not use a preposition but the French equivalent does (ex. *to need* — *avoir besoin* **de**); in others, the English preposition is placed so far from the pronoun that it is difficult to see the relationship of one with the other.

NOTES:

The selection of the interrogative pronoun after a preposition is more complicated. Remember that you must work with the preposition used in French and that you must change spoken English to formal English to help you determine function and to establish French word order (see pp. 82-83).

- *Here are three notebooks; **which (one)** do you need?*

    1. What noun is **which** referring to?
    Notebooks.

    2. What is the gender of *notebooks* in French?
    Cahiers is masculine.

    3. Select the gender of the pronoun that corresponds to the gender found under step 2:
    Lequel.

    4. Make the pronoun singular or plural depending on whether you want to say *which one* (singular) or *which ones* (plural).

    In this case it remains singular.

    5. Function: To determine the function, remember that *to need* is **avoir besoin de** *(to have need of).*

Which one do you need? → **Of which one* do you have need?
/
preposition

Which is the object of the preposition **de.**

    6. Add the preposition found under step 5 to the pronoun found under step 3:

---

de + lequel → **du**quel

Voici trois cahiers; **duquel** avez-vous besoin?

---

*An asterisk before a sentence means the sentence is ungrammatical. The purpose of including such a sentence is to compare it to the French one.

- *Here are four girls; **which (ones)** do you want to speak to?*

    1. What noun is **which** referring to?
    Girls.

    2. What is the gender of *girls* in French?
    Filles is feminine.

    3. Select the gender of the pronoun that corresponds to the gender found under step 2:
    Laquelle.

    4. Make the pronoun singular or plural depending on whether you want to say *which one* (singular) or *which ones* (plural):

    In this case it becomes plural: **lesquelles.**

    5. Function: To determine the function, change the structure of the question in English to one which will place the preposition within the sentence (see pp. 104-105).

Which ones do you want to speak *to*? → *To which ones* do you want to speak?

Remember that *to speak to* is **parler à.**
/
preposition

Which is the object of the preposition à.

    6. Add the preposition found under step 5 to the pronoun found under step 4.

à + lesquelles → auxquelles

Voici quatre filles; **auxquelles** voulez-vous parler?

<< What is a Demonstrative Pronoun? >>

A **demonstrative pronoun** replaces a noun which has been mentioned before. It is called demonstrative because it points out a person or thing. The word *demonstrative* comes from the same word as *demonstrate*, meaning *to point out*.

In English: The demonstrative pronouns are: *this*, meaning *this one*, and *that*, meaning *that one*, in the singular and *these* and *those* in the plural.

> Here are two suitcases. *This one* is big, and *that one* is small.

The distinction between *this* and *that* can be used to contrast one object from the other, or to refer to things that are not the same distance away. We generally say *this* for the closer object, and *that* for the one farther away.

In French: The demonstrative pronoun agrees in gender and number with the noun it replaces. To choose the correct form you should start by analyzing the noun replaced, **the antecedent**. Follow these steps:

1. Start by choosing the equivalent for *one* or *ones*.

    one   celui or celle

    • If the noun replaced is masculine singular:

    *Give me **the book**. This **one**.*
         /   /
       le livre   celui

    • If the noun replaced is feminine singular:

    *Give me **the letter**. That **one**.*
          /   /
       la lettre   celle

ones   ceux or **celles**

- If the noun replaced is masculine plural:

  *Give me **the books**. These (**ones**).*
        /   /
     les livres   ceux

- If the noun replaced is feminine plural:

  *Give me **the letters**. Those (**ones**).*
        /   /
     les lettres   celles

2. Now indicate *this* or *that* by adding -ci or -là after the pronoun chosen under step 1.

this   -ci

  *Give me the **book**. **This** one.*
  Celui-**ci**.

  *Give me the **letter**. **This** one.*
  Celle-**ci**.

  *Give me the **books**. **These** (ones).*
  Ceux-**ci**.

  *Give me the **letters**. **These** (ones).*
  Celles-**ci**.

that   -là

  *Give me the **book**. **That** one.*
  Celui-**là**.

  *Give me the **letter**. **That** one.*
  Celle-**là**.

  *Give me the **books**. **These** (ones).*
  Ceux-**là**.

  *Give me the **letters**. **Those** (ones).*
  Celles-**là**.

116

When choosing a demonstrative pronoun, follow these steps to find the correct form:

*Here are two suitcases. **This one** is big and **that one** is small.*

1. What noun is the pronoun replacing?
   Suitcases.
2. What is the gender of that noun in French?
   Valises is feminine.
3. Is the pronoun referring to one or more things?
   This one refers to one thing; therefore the pronoun will be singular. ***That one*** refers to one thing and will also be singular.
4. Selection: **celle-ci** *(this one),* **celle-là** *(that one).*

Voici deux valises. **Celle-ci** est grande; **celle-là** est petite.

There is another demonstrative pronoun which is being studied separately because it does not follow the same pattern.

In English: The demonstrative pronouns *the one* and *the ones*, unlike *this one* and *that one*, do not *point out* a specific object, but instead introduce a clause which helps us identify the object by giving additional information about a noun previously mentioned (location, owner, etc.).

What book are you reading?
The one (that) we bought yesterday.

Which dresses do you prefer?
The ones that are in front.

In French: The demonstrative pronoun *the one* and *the ones* agree in gender and number with the noun replaced. Moreover, the relative pronoun *that*, which is sometimes omitted in English, must be expressed in French and will change according to the function of the pronoun in the relative clause.

You will therefore have to select the demonstrative pronoun according to the first step outlined on pp. 114-115.
In addition, the correct relative pronoun will have to be
inserted as outlined in the section called **What is a Relative
Pronoun?** (see p. 126). The above two sentences in French
would read as follows:

> Quel livre lisez-vous?
>
> **Celui que** nous avons acheté hier.
>   /   /
> masc. sing.   *object of relative clause*

> Quelles robes préférez-vous?
>
> **Celles qui** sont devant.
>   /   /
> fém. pl.   *subject of relative clause*

These demonstrative pronouns *the one, the ones* are also
commonly used in a French structure which has no equivalent in English. For the same reason that clauses such as
"my father's house" can only be expressed in French with
the structure "the house of my father," you must use an
alternate structure to say the following:

- *Whose house are you living in?*

  My father's.

> The only structure you can use in French is *the
> one of my father.*

> | My father's → *the one of* my father. |
> | --- |

> *The one* depends on the gender and number of
> the noun it replaces *(the house)*. The French
> equivalent for *house* is **la maison** which is fem-
> inine singular.

> **Celle** de mon père.
>   /
> fém. sing.

118

- *Whose pens are you using?*
  My brother's.

> The only structure you can use in French is *the ones of my brother.*

My brother*'s* → ***the ones of*** my brother.

The gender and number of ***the ones*** depends on the gender and number of the noun it replaces *(the pens).* The French equivalent for *the pens* is **les stylos** which is masculine plural.

Ceux de mon frère.
　　/
masc. sing.

Be sure to rework these English structures before you write them in French.

———————

NOTES:

<< What is a Possessive Pronoun? >>

A **possessive pronoun** is a word which replaces a noun and which also shows who possesses that noun.

> Whose house is that?
> *Mine.*

Mine is a pronoun which replaces the noun *house* and which shows who possesses that noun.

In English: Possessive pronouns refer only to the person who possesses, not to the object possessed.

> Example 1.   Is that your house? Yes, it is *mine.*
> Example 2.   Are those your keys? Yes, they are *mine.*

The same possessive pronoun *mine* is used, although the object possessed is singular in Example 1 *(house)* and plural in Example 2 *(keys).*

Here is a list of the English possessive pronouns:

mine	ours
yours	yours
his, hers, its	theirs

The possessive pronoun refers to the person who possesses.

> John's car is blue. *His* is blue.
> Mary's car is green. *Hers* is green.

In French: The possessive pronoun refers to and describes the object which is possessed (not, as in English, to the person who possesses). Like all pronouns in French, the possessive pronoun must agree in number and gender with the noun it replaces. In addition, the possessive pronoun is preceded by the definite article which also agrees in gender and number with the object possessed. The complete list of possessive pronouns is not given here. You will need to consult your French grammar book.

120

Compare the agreement of possessive pronouns in English and in French:

Possessive form in French

English:	Is that ***Paul's*** house? Yes, it's ***his.***	
French:	Is that Paul's ***house***? Yes, it's ***his.***	la sienne

English:	Is that ***Jane's*** house? Yes, it's ***hers.***	
French:	Is that Jane's ***house***? Yes, it's ***hers.***	la sienne

English:	Is that ***Paul's*** book? Yes, it's ***his.***	
French:	Is that Paul's ***book***? Yes, it's ***his.***	le sien

English:	Is that ***Jane's*** book? Yes, it's ***hers.***	
French:	Is that Jane's ***book***? Yes, it's ***hers.***	le sien

A. The possessive pronouns for ***mine, yours*** (**tu** *form*) and ***his*** and ***hers*** each have a different masculine and feminine form in the singular and plural. You can find the correct possessive pronoun by following these steps.

1. Determine which definite article will precede the possessive pronoun by establishing the gender and number of the object possessed:

Definite article

- if the object possessed is masculine singular

  le livre   *book*   **le**

- if the object possessed is feminine singular

  la maison   *house*   **la**

- if the object possessed is plural

  les livres   *books*   **les**

  les maisons   *houses*

2. Indicate the possessor. In French, this will be shown by the first letter of the possessive pronoun:

mine	the first letter will be	**m-**
your **tu** *form*	the first letter will be	**t-**
his *hers* *its*	the first letter will be	**s-**

3. Fill in the possessive pronoun so that it will agree in gender and number with the object possessed. Start by analyzing the gender and number of the object possessed.

- If it is masculine singular, add **-ien**.

  C'est **le** livre. C'est **le mien.** *It is mine.*
  C'est **le tien.** *It is yours.*
  C'est **le sien.** *It is his./It is hers.*

- If it is feminine singular, add **-ienne**.

  C'est **la** lettre. C'est **la mienne.** *It is mine.*
  C'est **la tienne.** *It is yours.*
  C'est **la sienne.** *It is his.*
  It is hers.

- If it is masculine plural, add **-iens**.

  Ce sont **les** livres.
  Ce sont **les miens.** *They are mine.*
  Ce sont **les tiens.** *They are yours.*
  Ce sont **les siens.** *They are his.*
  They are hers.

- If it is feminine plural, add **-iennes**.

  Ce sont **les** lettres.
  Ce sont **les miennes.** *They are mine.*
  Ce sont **les tiennes.** *They are yours.*
  Ce sont **les siennes.** *They are his.*
  They are hers.

Let's apply these three steps to the following examples:

- *Whose book is that? It's **mine**.*

    Livre is masculine singular.

    1. Selection of definite article: **le**
    2. First letter of possessor: *mine* = m-
    3. Fill in to agree with object possessed: add -ien

    Completed pronoun: **mien**

    A qui est ce livre? C'est **le mien**.

- *Whose house is that? It's **his**.*

    Maison is feminine singular.

    1. Selection of definite article: **la**
    2. First letter of possessor: *his* = s-
    3. Fill in to agree with object possessed: add -ienne

    Completed pronoun: **sienne**

    A qui est cette maison? C'est **la sienne**.

- *Whose books are those? They are **hers**.*

    Livres is masculine plural.

    1. Selection of definite article: **les**
    2. First letter of possessor: *hers* = s-
    3. Fill in to agree with object possessed: add -iens

    Completed pronoun: **siens**

    A qui sont ces livres? Ce sont **les siens**.

- *Whose keys are those? They are **his**.*

    Clés is feminine plural.

    1. Selection of definite article: **les**
    2. First letter of possessor: *his* = s-
    3. Fill in to agree with
       object possessed: add **-iennes**

       Completed pronoun: **siennes**

    A qui sont les clés? Ce sont **les siennes**.

B. The possessive pronouns for ***ours, yours*** (**vous** *form*) and ***theirs*** have one form for the singular and one form for the plural, but there is no indication of gender. You can find the correct possessive pronoun by following these steps.

    1. Determine which definite article will precede the possessive pronoun by establishing the gender and number of the object possessed:

		Definite article
• if the object possessed is masculine singular		
le livre	*book*	**le**
• if the object possessed is feminine singular		
la maison	*house*	**la**
• if the object possessed is plural		
les livres	*books*	**les**
les maisons	*houses*	

2. Indicate the possessor and make it agree in number with the object possessed:

ours

- if the object possessed is singular   *Pronoun*

    This *house* is **ours**.   **nôtre**

- if the object possessed is plural

    These *houses* are **ours**.   **nôtres**

yours

- if the object possessed is singular

    This *book* is **yours**.   **vôtre**

- if the object possessed is plural

    These *books* are **yours**.   **vôtres**

theirs

- if the object possessed is singular

    This *book* is **theirs**.   **leur**

- if the object possessed is plural

    These *books* are **theirs**.   **leurs**

Let's apply these two steps to the following examples:

- *Whose book is that? It is **ours**.*

    Livre is masculine singular.

    1. Selection of definite article: **le**
    2. Indicate the possessor: ***ours* = nôtre**

    A qui est ce livre? C'est **le nôtre**.

- *Whose keys are those? They are **yours**.*

Clés is feminine plural.

    1. Selection of definite article: **les**

    2. Indicate the possessor: ***yours*** = **vôtres**

A qui sont ces clés? Ce sont **les vôtres.**

NOTES:

<< What is a Relative Pronoun? >>

A **relative pronoun** is a word that serves two purposes:

1. As a pronoun it stands for a noun or another pronoun previously mentioned (called its **antecedent**).

   This is the boy *who* broke the window.
   /
   antecedent

2. It introduces a **subordinate clause**; that is, a group of words having a subject and verb separate from the main subject and verb of the sentence.

   This is the boy *who broke the window.*
   /   /
   main clause   subordinate clause

   The above subordinate clause is also called a **relative clause** because it starts with a relative pronoun *(who)*. The relative clause gives us additional information about the antecedent *(boy)*.

In English and in French, the relative pronoun used will depend on the function of the relative pronoun in the relative clause. You must train yourself to go through the following steps:

1. Find the relative clause.
2. Determine the function of the relative pronoun in the relative clause.
   - Is it the subject?
   - Is it the object?
3. Select the pronoun according to the antecedent.
   - Is it a person?
   - Is it a thing?

In English: Here are the English relative pronouns.

<u>Subject of the relative clause:</u>

- *who* (if the antecedent is a person)

  This is the student *who* answered.
  /
  antecedent

  Who is the subject of *answered.*

- *which* (if the antecedent is a thing)

  This is the book *which* is so popular.
  /
  antecedent

  Which is the subject of *is.*

- *that* (if the antecedent is a person or a thing)

  This is the student *that* answered.
  /
  antecedent

  That is the subject of *answered.*

  This is the book *that* is so popular.
  /
  antecedent

  That is the subject of *is.*

128

<u>Object of the relative clause</u>: These pronouns are often omitted in English. We have indicated them in parentheses because they must be expressed in French.

- *whom*   (if the antecedent is a person)

  This is the student *(whom)* I saw.
  /
  antecedent

  Whom is the direct object of *saw*.

- *which*   (if the antecedent is a thing)

  This is the book *(which)* I bought.
  /   /
  antecedent   subject of relative clause

  Which is the direct object of *bought*.

- *that*   (if the antecedent is a person or a thing)

  This is the student *(that)* I saw.
  /   /
  antecedent   subject of relative clause

  That is the direct object of *saw*.

  This is the book *(that)* I read.
  /   /
  antecedent   subject of relative clause

  That is the direct object of *read*.

These relative pronouns enable you to combine two sentences into one. Look at the following examples:

- Sentence A: That is the boy.

  Sentence B: He broke the window.

  You can combine Sentence A and Sentence B by replacing the subject pronoun *he* with the relative pronoun **who**.

  That is the boy **who** *broke the window.*

  Who broke the window is the **relative clause.** It does not express a complete thought and it is introduced by a relative pronoun.

  Who stands for the noun *boy*, so that *boy* is called the **antecedent** of **who**. Notice that the antecedent stands immediately before the pronoun which gives additional information about it.

  Who serves as the subject of the verb *broke* in the relative clause *who broke the window.*

- Sentence A: The French teacher is nice.

  Sentence B: I met her today.

  You can combine Sentence A and Sentence B by replacing the object pronoun *her* with the relative pronoun **whom**.

  The French teacher, **whom** *I met today*, is nice.

  Whom I met today is the relative clause.

  Whom stands for the noun *teacher*, so that *teacher* is the antecedent. Notice again that the antecedent comes immediately before the relative pronoun.

  Whom serves as the direct object of the relative clause. (*"I"* is the subject.)

130

- Sentence A: Here is the student.

  Sentence B: I am speaking to him.

You can combine Sentence A and Sentence B by replacing the indirect object pronoun *to him* with the relative pronoun *to whom.*

In spoken English, you would combine these two sentences by saying: "Here is the student I am speaking to." This structure will have to be changed.

Take the preposition *to* at the end of the sentence and place it within the sentence. In order to include *to* within the sentence you will have to add the relative pronoun *whom.*

Here is the student I am speaking *to.* → Here is the student *to whom* I am speaking.

Restructuring these sentences will help you identify the relative clause and will give you the French word order (see pp. 82-83).

Here is the student *to whom I am speaking.*

To whom I am speaking is the relative clause.

Whom stands for the student, so that *student* is the antecedent.

Notice that the only word that separates *whom* from its antecedent is the preposition. That preposition is the clue that the relative pronoun is <u>not</u> a direct object but an indirect object. (*"I"* is the subject.)

In French: To find the correct relative pronoun you must go through the following steps:

1. Find the relative clause and separate it from the rest of the sentence.

2. Determine the function of the relative pronoun in the relative clause.

3. Select the pronoun according to the antecedent.

Subject of the relative clause:

- **qui** (if the antecedent is a person or thing)

This is the *student who* answered.
/
In French : **qui**

This is the *book which* is so popular.
/
In French : **qui**

Direct object of the relative clause: These relative pronouns are sometimes omitted in English. They must be expressed in French.

- **que** (if the antecedent is a person or thing)

This is the *student (whom)* I saw.
/
In French : **que**

This is the *book (which)* I bought.
/
In French : **que**

The next two functions involve prepositions. Make sure that you work with the preposition used in French and that you place the preposition within the sentence.

132

Object of the preposition **de**:

- **dont**   (if the antecedent is a person or thing)

This is the book *(that)* I need.
Remember that *to need* is **avoir besoin de.**

This is the *book (that)* I need. → This is the *book of which* I have need.

This is the book *(that)* I need.
/
In French : **dont**

- **de qui**   (if the antecedent is a person)

This is the man *(that)* I'm speaking about.
Remember that *to speak about* is **parler de.**

This is the *man (that)* I'm speaking *about.* → This is the *man about whom*
I am speaking.

This is the man *(that)* I'm speaking *about.*
/
In French : **de qui**

Object of any other preposition (besides **de**):

- preposition + **lequel**   (if the antecedent is a person
  or thing)

Lequel must agree with antecedent in gender and
number (see p. 110).

These are the pens *(that)* I write with.

These are the *pens (that)* I write *with.* → These are the *pens with which*
I write.

These are the pens *(that)* I write *with.*
/
In French : **avec lesquels**

This is the man *(that)* I'm thinking about.

This is the *man (that)* I'm thinking *about.* → This is the *man about whom* I'm thinking.

This is the man *(that)* I'm thinking *about.*

In French : ┌ à + lequel → auquel ┐

- preposition + **qui**   (if the antecedent is a person)

This is the man *(that)* I'm thinking *about.*

In French : à **qui**

Let's apply the steps outlined above to the following sentences in order to select the correct relative pronoun:

- *The plane **that** comes from New York is late.*

    1. Relative clause: *that comes from New York*
    2. Function of *that*: Subject of relative clause
    3. Selection: **qui**

L'avion **qui** arrive de New York est en retard.

- *Here are the books **(that)** I bought yesterday.*

    1. Relative clause: *that I bought yesterday*
    2. Function of *that*: Direct object of relative clause
    3. Selection: **que**

Voici les livres **que** j'ai achetés hier.

Notice the agreement of past participle **achetés** with the direct object **livres** (see p. 45).

● *Where is the book (that) you need.*

Remember that *to need* is **avoir besoin de** (to
have need *of*).　　　　　　　　　　**preposition**

Since this sentence involves a preposition **de**, be
sure to place it within the sentence.

Where is the book *(that)* you need? → Where is the book *of which* you
have need?

---

1. Relative clause: *of which you have need*
2. Function of *which*: object of the preposition **de**
3. Selection: **dont**

Où est le livre **dont** vous avez besoin?

● *Where is the letter (that) she's thinking about?*
　　　　　　　　　　　　　　　　　　preposition

Since this sentence involves a preposition, be
sure to place it within the sentence.

Where is the *letter (that)* she's thinking *about?* → Where is the *letter
about which* she is thinking?

---

1. Relative clause: *about which she is thinking*
   Remember that *to think about* is **penser à**.
2. Function of *which*: object of the preposition **à**
3. Selection: **à laquelle** (antecedent: **la lettre**)
   　　　fém. sing.　　　　　　　　　fém. sing.

Où est la lettre **à laquelle** elle pense.

- *That is the boy (that) she's playing **with**.*

  /
  preposition

  Since this sentence involves a preposition, be sure to place it within the sentence.

That is the *boy (that)* she's playing *with.* → That is the *boy with whom* she is playing.

---

1. Relative clause: *with whom she is playing*
2. Function of ***whom***: object of the preposition
   with
   /
   avec
3. Selection: **avec lequel** (antecedent: **le garçon**)
   /   /
   masc. sing.   masc. sing.

   or   **avec qui** (antecedent: **le garçon**)
   /
   a person

Voici le garçon **avec lequel** elle joue.

Voici le garçon **avec qui** elle joue.

Relative pronouns are difficult to handle and this handbook provides only a simple outline. Refer to your French grammar book for additional rules.

NOTES:

136

<< What are Relative Pronouns without Antecedents? >>

The **relative pronouns** without antecedents are pronouns used instead of a noun which has <u>not</u> been expressed, so that there is no antecedent.

In English: The word *what* meaning *that which* occurs without an antecedent.

Compare these sentences:

Here is the book *(that)* I read.
/
antecedent : book

Here is *what* I read.
/
no antecedent

This is *what* happened.
/
no antecedent

It's easy to see that there is no antecedent, because antecedents come just before relative pronouns.

The pronoun *what* (meaning *that which*) should not be confused with other uses of *what*, such as *what* as an interrogative pronoun (*What do you want?* **Qu'est-ce que** vous voulez? See p. 103) and *what* as an interrogative adjective (*What book do you want?* **Quel** livre voulez-vous? See p. 75).

In French: The pronoun **ce** (which is considered masculine singular) functions as the antecedent. It is followed by whatever relative pronoun would have been used if there had been a noun antecedent.

To find the correct form of the pronoun, follow the same steps you used to find relative pronouns with antecedents (see pp. 131-133). They are summarized below:

1. Find the relative clause and separate it from the rest of the sentence.

2. Determine the function of the relative pronoun in the relative clause.
   - Subject of the relative clause: **qui**
   - Direct object of the relative clause: **que**
   - Object of the preposition **de**:
     When referring to a person   **de qui**
     When referring to a thing   **dont** or **de quoi**
     (omit step 3)
   - Object of any other preposition besides **de**:
     When referring to a person   preposition + **qui**
     When referring to a thing   preposition + **quoi**

3. Add the word **ce** before the pronoun selected under step 2. (This is optional before an object of any preposition besides **de** above.)

Let's apply the steps outlined above to the following sentences in order to select the correct relative pronoun.

- *Here is **what** happened.*
   1. Relative clause: *what happened*
   2. Function of **what**: subject of *happened*
   3. Selection: **qui**
   4. Add **ce**: **ce qui**

   Voici **ce qui** est arrivé.

- *Show me **what** you bought.*
   1. Relative clause: *what you bought*
   2. Function of **what**: direct object of *bought*
   3. Selection: **que**
   4. Add **ce**: **ce que**

   Montrez-moi **ce que** vous avez acheté.

The selection of the relative pronoun, with or without an antecedent, is more complicated after a preposition. Remember that you must work with the preposition used in French and that you must place that preposition within the sentence to help you determine function and to establish French word order (see p. 82).

- *I don't know **what** he is talking about.*

    1. Relative clause: *what he is talking about*

    2. Function of ***what***: To determine the function, change the structure of the relative clause so that the preposition is not at the end of the clause.

    ---

    what he is talking *about* → *about what* he is talking

    Remember that ***to talk about*** is **parler de.**
    /
    preposition

    What is the object of the preposition **de.**

    3. Selection: **dont** or **de quoi** (without **ce**)

    4. Add **ce**: **ce dont**

Je ne sais pas **ce dont** il parle.
Je ne sais pas **de quoi** il parle.

- *I don't know **what** he is thinking about.*

  1. Relative clause: *what he is thinking about*

  2. Function of **what**: To determine the function, change the structure of the relative clause so that the preposition is not at the end of the clause.

  > *what* he is thinking *about* → *about what* he is thinking

  Remember that *to think about* is **penser à.**

  preposition

  What is the object of the preposition **à.**

  3. Selection: **à quoi**

  4. Add **ce** optional: **(ce) à quoi**

  Je ne sais pas **ce à quoi** il pense.

Relative pronouns are difficult to handle and this handbook provides only a simple outline. Refer to your French grammar book for additional rules.

<< Index >>

a, an   9, 10
active voice   64-67
adjective   68-70
   demonstrative   68, 78-79
   descriptive   68-69
   interrogative   68, 75-77
   noun used as   4, 69-70, 83
   possessive   68, 70-74
adverb   16, 79-81
   to change meaning of verbs   16
agent   64, 65
agreement   10
   adjective with noun   69, 71-81
   see also all headings under
   adjective
   noun and article   10
   past participle   45, 49, 63, 65
   pronoun with antecedent   23,
     94-97, 99, 101, 105, 110,
     114, 119-121, 132-133
aller (to go)   51, 52
to answer (**répondre à**)   91
antecedent   21, 114, 126, 129,
   137 *see also all headings*
   under pronoun
article (definite/indefinite)   9-12
to ask (**demander à**)   82, 90
auxiliary verb (helping verb)   17,
   19-20, 38-45 *see also* **avoir**
   and **être**
avoir (to have)   18-19, 38-40,
   45-46, 49, 53, 57

to be *see* **être**

ce   136-139
clause   56
   "if"   56-59
   main   56, 126
   relative   126, 129, 131-135,
     137-139
   result   56-59
   subordinate   56, 126
command form (**impératif**)   31
common noun   3-5, 7, 8
conditional (**conditionnel**)   31,
   55-60
   past (**conditionnel passé**)   56-59
   present (**conditionnel présent**)
     55, 57-60
   as polite form   57
   future in the past   56, 60
   hypothetical statement   56
conjugation   17, 25-30
conjunction   83
contrary-to-fact statement   61

de   14, 70, 83-84, 132, 134,
   137-138
declarative sentence   35
definite article   9-12
demonstrative adjective   68, 78-79
demonstrative pronoun   22, 114-
   118
descriptive adjective   68-69
direct object *see* object, direct
disjunctive pronoun (**pronom**
   personnel tonique)   22, 99-
   102

141